CW01158062

Flowering Bulbs
for the garden

KEW GARDENING GUIDES

Flowering Bulbs
for the garden

Brian Mathew

Series editor John Simmons
M. Hort. (RHS), F.I.Hort., C.Biol., M.I.Biol.

The Royal Botanic Gardens, Kew
in association with
COLLINGRIDGE

Front cover photograph: S. and O. Mathews
Back cover photograph: Jerry Harpur (Garsington Manor)

Published in 1987 by Collingridge Books,
an imprint of The Hamlyn Publishing Group Limited,
Bridge House, 69 London Road, Twickenham, Middlesex, England
in association with The Royal Botanic Gardens, Kew.

Copyright © The Hamlyn Publishing Group Limited 1987

All rights reserved. No part of this publication may be
reproduced, stored in a retrieval system, or transmitted, in
any form or by any means, electronic, mechanical, photocopying,
recording or otherwise, without the prior permission of The
Hamlyn Publishing Group Limited.

Second impression 1987

ISBN 0 600 35175 0

Filmset in England by Vision Typesetting, Manchester
in 11 on 12 pt Bembo

Printed in Hong Kong by
Mandarin Offset

Contents

	Preface	11
	Foreword	12
	Introduction	13
1	*The History and Conservation of Bulbs*	15
2	*Bulbous Plants in the Wild*	21
3	*The Principles of Bulb Growing*	27
4	*Flowering Bulbs around the Garden*	31
5	*Special Bulbs for the Enthusiast*	53
	A to Z of Flowering Bulbs	59
	Bulbs for Selected Sites	115
	Glossary	119
	Acknowledgements	121
	Bibliography	122
	Index	123

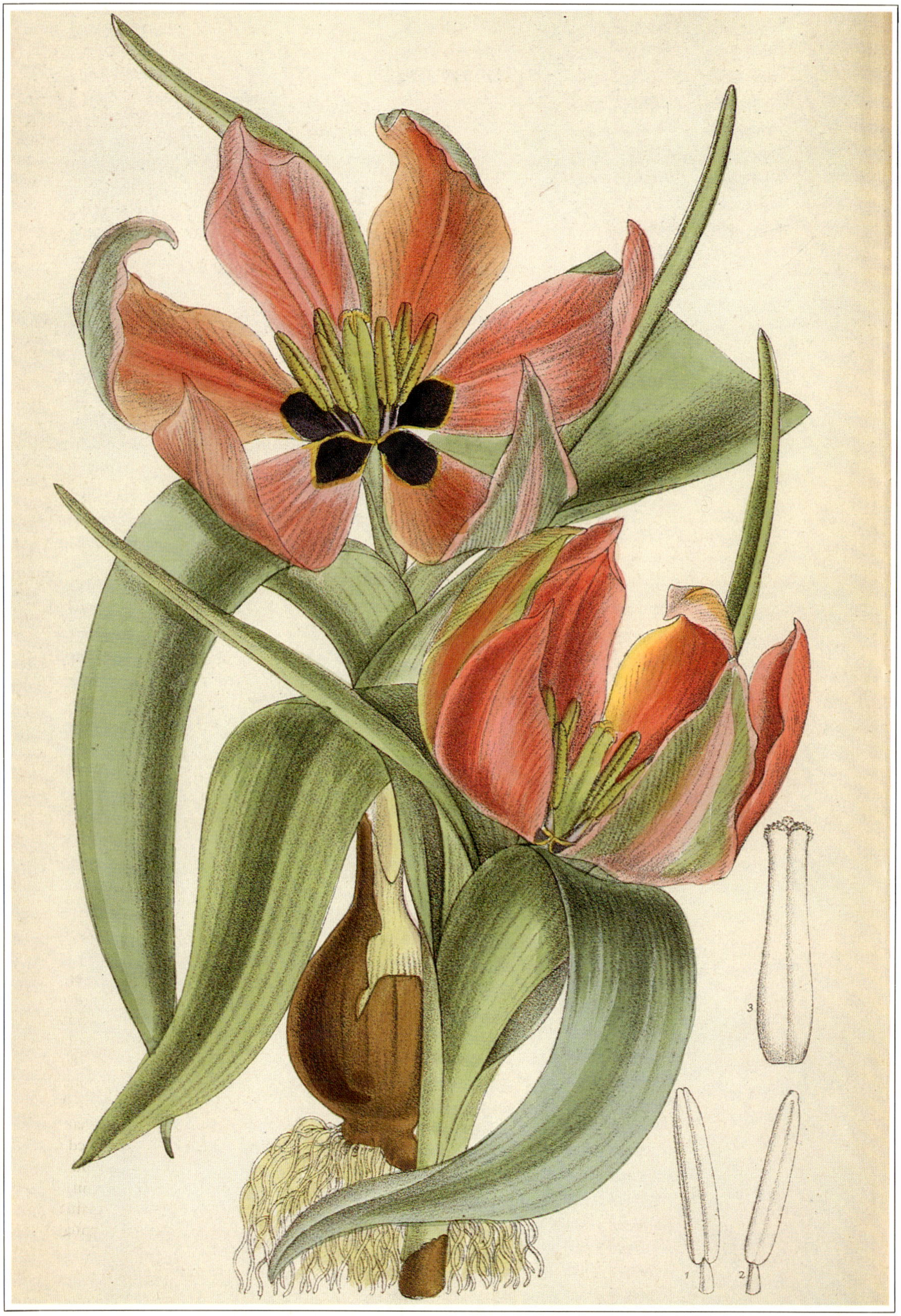
3
1
2

Preface

The Royal Botanic Gardens, Kew with their herbarium, library, laboratories and unrivalled collection of living plants, form one of the world's most important centres of botanical science. Their origins, however, can be traced back to a modest nine-acre site in the Pleasure Garden at Kew which Augusta, the Dowager Princess of Wales and mother of King George III, set aside for the cultivation of new and interesting plants.

On this site were grown many of the exotic species which reached England for the first time during this period of mercantile and colonial expansion. Trees such as our oldest specimens of *Sophora japonica* from China and *Robinia pseudoacacia* from America were planted for the Princess and still flourish at Kew, as do many accessions from Africa and Australia.

Many of Kew's earliest collectors were botanical explorers who made difficult and dangerous journeys to remote and unknown parts of the world in their search for economically important or beautiful plants. The work of Kew's botanists in gathering new species was complemented by that of Kew's gardeners, who were responsible for their care and propagation. The gardeners were also responsible for trans-shipping living plants from Kew to other parts of the world, and the Gardens rapidly became a clearing house through which 'useful' species grown in one continent were transferred to another.

At the present time, the living collections of the Royal Botanic Gardens contain approximately 50,000 types of flowering plants from every corner of the earth. Such a collection makes unending demands on the skills and dedication of those entrusted with its care. It also provides an unrivalled opportunity for gardening staff to familiarize themselves with the diverse requirements of plants from the many different climatic and geological regions of the world. The plants in the Royal Botanic Gardens are no museum collection, however. As in the eighteenth and nineteenth centuries, the Gardens continue to distribute living plant material on a worldwide basis, though they now use modern facilities such as the micropropagation unit at Kew and the Seed Bank at Wakehurst Place. The Gardens are also actively involved in the conservation of the world's plant resources and in supplying scientists at Kew and elsewhere with the plants and plant material required for their research. This may range from basic studies of the ways in which plants have evolved to the isolation of plant chemicals of potential use in agriculture and medicine. Whatever the purpose of the research, there is inevitably a need to grow plants and to grow them well, whether they be plants from the rain forests of the Amazon or from the deserts of Africa.

Your interest in gardening may be neither scientific nor economic, but I believe that the expert advice provided by specialist authors in this new series of *Kew Gardening Guides* will provide help of a quality that can be given only by gardeners with long experience of the art and science of cultivating a particular group of plants.

E. Arthur Bell
Director, Royal Botanic Gardens, Kew

Opposite:
Tulipa sintenisii was given its present botanical name in 1891, but is probably one of the Asiatic species that were introduced much earlier and resulted in tulipomania in the seventeenth century

Foreword

Gardening is in part instinctive, in part experience. Look in any village or town and you will see many gardens, balconies or even windowsills full of healthy plants brightening up the streets. However, there are always likely to be other plots that are sterile and devoid of plants, or overgrown and unloved. Admittedly gardening is laborious, but the hours spent sweating behind a mower on a hot summer's day will be amply rewarded when the smooth green lawn is admired; the painful nettle stings incurred while clearing ground will soon be forgotten when the buds of newly planted shrubs burst forth in spring.

These few examples of the joy and pain of gardening are all part of its attraction to its devotees. The successful gardeners and plant lovers of this world come to understand plants instinctively, learning their likes and dislikes, their lifespan and ultimate size, recognizing and correcting ailments before they become serious. They work with the seasons of the year, not against them; they think ahead, driven by caring, being aware of when conditions are right for planting, mowing or harvesting and, perhaps most important of all, they know when to leave well alone.

This understanding of the natural order cannot be learned overnight. It is a continuous two-way process that lasts a lifetime. In creating a garden, past masters such as Humphry Repton in the eighteenth century or Gertrude Jekyll in the nineteenth perceived and enhanced the natural advantages of a site, and Jekyll in particular was an acute observer of the countryside and its seasons. Seeing a plant in its natural situation gives knowledge of its needs in cultivation. And then, once design and planting have formed a garden, the process reverses as the garden becomes the inspiration for learning about the natural world.

With the widespread loss of the world's natural habitats now causing the daily extinction of species, botanic gardens and other specialist gardens are becoming as arks, holding irreplaceable collections. Thus gardens are increasingly cooperating to form networks which can retain as great a diversity of plants as possible. More than ever gardens can offer a refuge for our beleaguered flora and fauna and, whether a garden be great or small, formal or natural, this need should underpin its enduring qualities of peace and harmony – the challenge of the creative unison of formal and natural areas.

The authors of these volumes have all become acknowledged specialists in particular aspects of gardening and their texts draw on their experience and impart the vitality that sustains their own enthusiasm and dedication. It is hoped, therefore, that these *Kew Gardening Guides* will be the means of sharing their hard-earned knowledge and understanding with a wider audience.

Like a many faceted gemstone, horticulture has many sides, each with its own devotees, but plants are the common link, and they define this series of horticultural books and the work of Kew itself.

John Simmons
Editor

Introduction

The author of a book on bulbs has an immediate problem when putting pen to paper, and that is to explain what the content of his work is to be. The term bulb in its botanical sense is limited to an organ which consists of separate scales attached to a fleshy basal core. This of course includes many well-known plants such as daffodils, lilies, amaryllis, snowdrops and a good household example, the onion, but 'bulb' excludes a host of others, such as crocus and gladiolus, which have corms. The corm is a solid, non-scaly structure, which is replaced each year by a new one and is covered with a series of fibrous coats. Other plants, such as cyclamen and some anemones, have tubers, which are solid underground organs without any covering. Nevertheless, all these are lumped together into nurserymen's bulb catalogues. The subjects which are to be found in the autumn catalogues each year, loosely termed as bulbs, really include any plants which can be dug up, dried off and sold in packets – any plant, in fact, which has a swollen underground storage organ. However, no author in his right mind would attempt to write and sell a book entitled *Underground Storage Organs for the Garden*; there is no all-embracing term for these plants, and the only usable word which most people will understand is 'bulb'. So, readers of this book will find not only bulbs in the botanical sense but all the other types of plant which can spend at least part of their life cycle in a neatly packaged form without any visibly active growing parts. I use the word 'visibly' because even in the dormant bulb there is usually something going on at its centre, such as the formation of buds for the coming season.

The book is intended to be an overall guide to the cultivation of bulbs, giving details of how and where they may be used in the garden, how to increase them and how to prevent pests and diseases from decreasing them, followed by an A to Z of the most successful and popular species and their garden forms. It is, however, before considering their horticultural value, worth looking briefly, in Chapter 1, at bulbs in their wild state and, in Chapter 2, at how this knowledge has a bearing on the way in which we try to grow them in our gardens.

The book is primarily intended for outdoor gardeners and the main sections deal with the type of garden situations in which bulbs can be planted successfully, followed by descriptions of the plants themselves. We have not gone into the rather more specialized field of growing tropical or tender bulbs in the protection of heated glasshouses, though there is a section devoted to the cultivation of bulbs in containers for decorating a terrace or patio, and another in which we take a look at the value of an unheated frame or greenhouse for growing some of the slightly more tricky groups of bulbs.

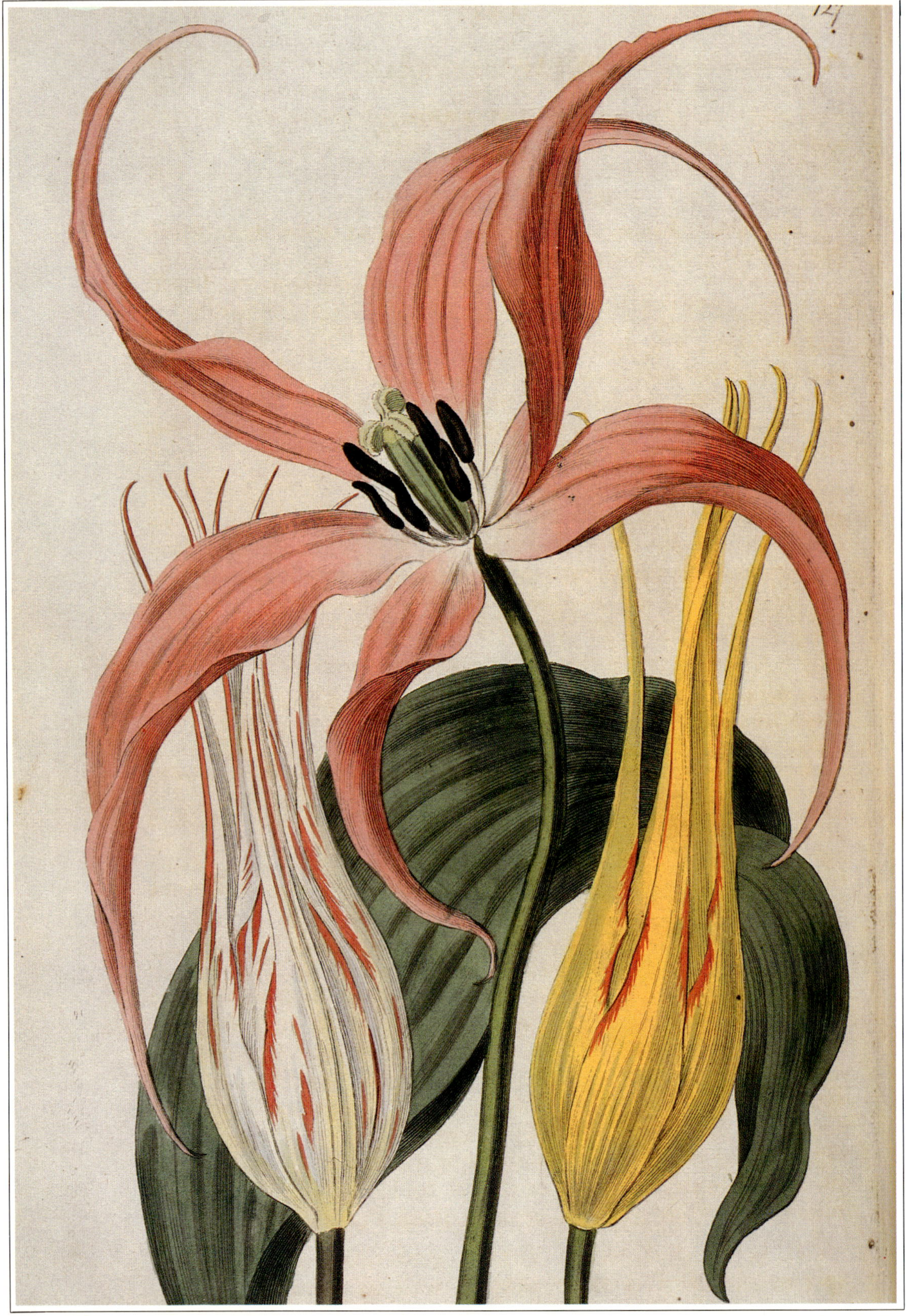

1
The History and Conservation of Bulbs

The current peak in popularity of bulbous plants is not a new phenomenon, for there have been other occasions in the past when their following has become something of a cult. Various boom times have occurred, undoubtedly one of the greatest being in the sixteenth century when such exciting species as tulips, hyacinths and crown imperials were 'discovered' in the gardens of the Ottoman Turks by European travellers such as Busbecq.

THE EARLY COLLECTORS

They were introduced into western horticulture to form the basis of a vast industry which continues, notably in the Netherlands, to this day. There is evidence that the early Turkish horticulturists did collect bulbs from the wild with which to adorn their gardens, but it seems that they mainly concentrated on 'improving' the species in cultivation by selection and hybridization to produce a wider range of colours, shapes and sizes and, in the case of hyacinths, both single and double forms. Much has been written about tulips and the tulipomania that spread through Europe in the sixteenth and seventeenth centuries following these introductions, and this is not a suitable place to repeat this long but fascinating story. It is, however, interesting to note how sophisticated was the horticultural scene in Istanbul during the Ottoman period. New tulip varieties were brought before committees who awarded certificates, much as they are today by the various societies around the world. They were given cultivar names and these, and the hyacinth varieties, were recorded by artists whose work survives to this day in the Topkapi Museum in Istanbul. In the 1630s it is recorded that there were three hundred florists in Istanbul, and during the height of popularity of the tulip about 1500 varieties were known. Rare varieties could change hands for between 500 and 1000 gold coins. The 'boom' that started in the sixteenth century has in Europe lasted throughout the centuries to the present day, while interest in bulbs, indeed in gardening as a whole, has largely died out in the eastern countries where it originated. The great industry that arose as a result of the early introductions has been largely confined to raising bigger and better flowers in a wider range of colours in just a few genera, notably *Tulipa*, *Hyacinthus* and *Narcissus*, with a few other groups such as *Iris* and *Crocus* also attracting some attention. The degree of interest in wild species, on the other hand, has certainly had ups and downs but today we are very much at a peak, and the current enthusiasm for the obscure and unusual has resulted in the introduction of a great majority of the world's hardy bulb species, and a proliferation of small specialist nurseries. In fact I am sure that there are far more species of bulb presently in cultivation than there have been at any other time, though quite a lot of these are in a few specialist hands and may never become plentiful enough to reach the nursery trade. In view of all the enthusiasm it is easy to be led into believing that we are now doing things better than ever before, but

Opposite:
Tulipa cornuta from the *Botanical Register* of 1816. This elegant tulip is typical of those favoured by the Ottoman Turks in Istanbul in the sixteenth century. The nearest we have today is known as *T. acuminata*

Portrait of Edmund Boissier, author of *Flora Orientalis*

this is not necessarily so. There was a similar peak of interest in wild species in the mid-nineteenth to the early twentieth centuries, and it is worth noting a few of the famous names behind this period of 'bulbitis'.

William Herbert, who studied *Crocus*, hybridized *Gladiolus* species and made an exhaustive study of the Amaryllidaceae, was one of those who bridged the gap between botanists and gardeners, and whose work was of such a calibre that we still refer to it today, while in the botanical field J.G. Baker of Kew described and classified numerous 'bulbous' plants from all over the world. Edmund Boissier, whose important herbarium is preserved in Geneva, concentrated mainly on Mediterranean and western Asiatic plants and his *Flora Orientalis* is one of the starting points for any study of the flora of these regions. Other notable botanical personalities concerned with Asiatic bulbous plants in this period were H.K. Haussknecht, Eduard and Albert Regel, Karl Koch and Paul Sintenis. Botanists and horticulturists relied largely on the material sent back by avid explorers such as Theodor Kotschy, Walter Siehe and Edward Whittall, and some of the famous nurseries of the time employed collectors to introduce novelties for them. The nursery firms of van Tubergen, Hoog, Dammann, Barr, Krelage and many others were important outlets for these new and exciting plants, and one sees it as a golden period for gardeners and botanists alike, each no doubt stimulating the other. It is sobering to our egos when we enthusiastically view a solitary specimen of a rarity such as *Iris kolpakowskiana* only to find that a clump of it was illustrated in the *Botanical Magazine* of 1880!

Undoubtedly the fall in popularity after this rich period came with the onset of two world wars, when many species must have been lost through lack of attention, and it is only in the last two or three decades that the boom time has returned once more. The scene can, however, change rapidly and we have already lost a number of the species introduced in the 1960s and 1970s, when plant-hunting expeditions roamed freely in the bulb-rich lands of Iran and Afghanistan, areas which are now more or less closed to outsiders for the purposes of exploration.

I have concentrated my comments mainly on these regions since this is where the majority of the hardy bulbs for our gardens originate. A look at the more tender bulbs would result in rather different comments, with a peak of interest in the late eighteenth to early nineteenth centuries, when collectors and botanists such as Francis Masson and Carl Thunberg visited southern Africa and sent back seeds and specimens of, among other things, extraordinary new bulbous plants that became very popular in spite of the need for cultivation under glass. Today these are scarcely known by gardeners, and are really just in the hands of a few specialist amateurs and botanic gardens, and there are almost no commercial outlets. Such peaks and troughs of popularity for differing plant goups are probably inevitable for a variety of reasons, including pure whim, but it is sad that during the troughs species that may well have taken a great deal of time, effort and money to introduce are lost to cultivation. We should as insurance, therefore, make every effort as individuals to propagate and distribute our plants to others and never be in a position to boast that 'I have the only one!'

Collection and conservation

It would appear that on the whole the interest in bulbs during earlier times was in the improved types, not the wild species. Bulb collecting on a very large scale is probably a fairly modern trait, restricted mainly to the last hundred years, and much of the gathering of wild stocks has taken place during this period, coupled of course with a not inconsiderable amount of habitat destruction. The awareness by the general public of a need for conservation is quite new. Between fifty and a hundred years ago there was little thought given to the matter; either wild resources were thought to be quite boundless or, more likely, it just did not occur to most people that there was any value in preserving plants. Bulbs are particularly vulnerable, as they are easy to collect and transport during their dormant period; towards the end of the nineteenth and in the early twentieth centuries collecting of bulbs was carried out on a vast scale in places as far apart as Turkey and California, Chile and Central Asia, the local population sometimes being employed to work systematically through colonies of bulbs to clear an area. Today the position is perhaps slightly better, in that some countries have created reserves for the protection of wildlife while others impose fines even for picking the flowers of certain species, and international agreements prevent the movement of wild collected plants from one country to another. There is, however, still a large amount of commercial collecting in certain countries which are rich in bulbs, and these areas also attract the enthusiast who is interested in only a few bulbs of each species.

A warning for the future
This at first appears to be fairly innocent, but it must be remembered that it is usually the rarer species that interest the specialist, and several over enthusiastic people can soon decimate a small population of some local endemic species. It

would be sad to see all forms of collecting totally banned, but this is quite likely to be the outcome if we do not rapidly cut down on our exploitation of the world's flora. It would be even sadder if future generations looked back on our century as a time of wanton destruction, but this is the way we are heading. In this book we are concerned with the world of bulbous plants. The extinction of some of these species would not be devastating, however regrettable, and there is only a slight possibility that something of medicinal value would be lost, but it is the destruction of our own environment, the green plants and especially forests which moderate and even create our climate, that should really worry us. This extreme is only an extension of what we are already doing. But to return from this tragic affair to our bulbs. One must in this case take a reasoned view of the situation and in certain instances concerning bulbous plants I think that some of man's activities, such as felling of woodland and overgrazing, may have led to an increase in the area of distribution, and in consequence the numbers of individuals, of particular species. Shade-loving plants are adapted to living in habitats where the sunlight is reduced and humidity is reasonably high – in fact in these conditions some take to an epiphytic life on the branches of trees. Remove this protective canopy and the sun will soon dry out and kill the shade-lovers, the soil may be washed away and in severe cases, where deforestation is on a large scale, the water cycle may be interrupted and the whole climate made drier. Bulbous plants, on the other hand, have evolved a storage system to help them to overcome dry climatic periods. Their natural distribution was, in the early days of their development, almost certainly restricted to open habitats where there were long hot, dry spells, the effects of which could be avoided by plants dying down for a prolonged period of dormancy.

Natural selection
Such plants are thus capable of benefiting from the removal of any shade, and it seems very likely that in several countries of the Near and Middle East removal of woodland has resulted in expanding populations of certain species of bulbous plant at the expense of others. In the western United States it has been shown that felling of the forests has allowed populations of iris species to spread, merge and hybridize to such an extent that the identity of the original parents has been almost lost; such a 'melting pot' may in future lead to new species segregating out by genetic combinations which were not previously possible. Such a process may to some extent be repeating, in an accelerated way, the natural system of ebb and flow as climates change, as in ice ages for example, over the millennia. Alternating periods of isolation and stability followed by expansion and hybridization must surely be at least part of the answer to the wealth of species on our planet today, and this process continues, sometimes with man's unwitting assistance by encouraging the liaison between species that would otherwise be separated from each other. I would not like to give the impression that I regard the destruction of the flora as part of natural change. I certainly do not approve of the collecting of wild species for financial gain. Few of the tens of thousands of cyclamen, snowdrops or orchids removed each year from the wild survive for long. The nursery-grown product is bound to be best, especially if raised from seed. Inherent in all species is the ability to vary, and it is this that we need to exploit if we are to obtain the best results in our gardens. In the course of raising

seedlings those that are unsuited to our climate will be most likely to perish, while the most fitted will stand the best chance of survival; several generations of this process should produce a race of home grown plants tolerant of the local conditions – which conversely might well not survive if planted back in their original homeland! By all means introduce a nucleus stock of the newly discovered species to cultivation, and selected wild forms of already known species, but we must never regard the wild as our nursery to plunder until there is nothing left for future generations to see.

Gladiolus byzantinus. This wild species is found growing in the Mediterranean area

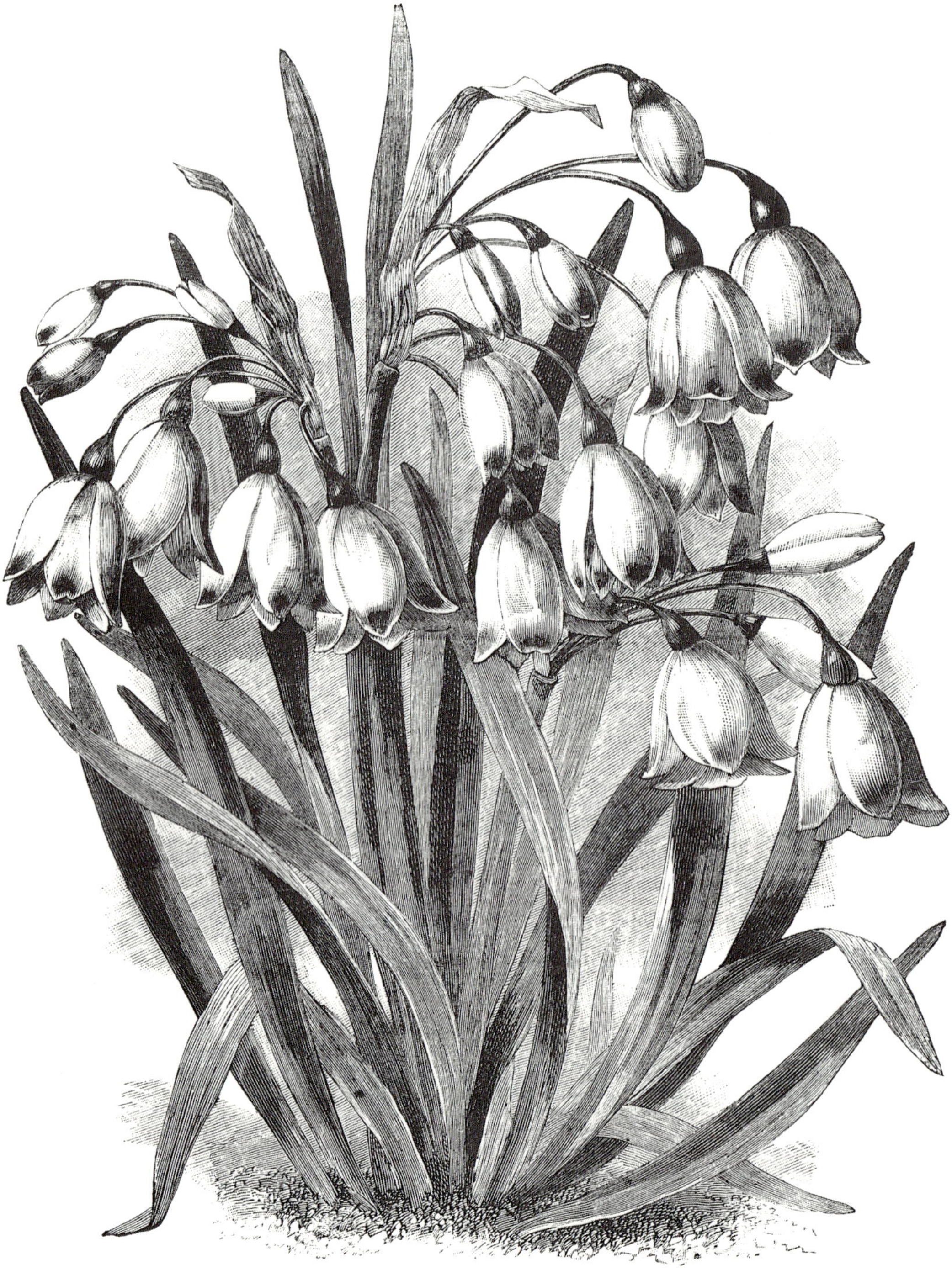

2
Bulbous Plants in the Wild

It is not only interesting to know the origins of the plants we grow in our gardens; it also has a practical direct link to the way in which we grow them. As a silly extreme example, the waterlily has evolved in a watery environment and no one in his right mind would attempt to grow it in the herbaceous border; similarly, bulbs have arrived at their state of development by adapting to certain climatic conditions and an understanding of these will help in the overall feeling we have for their cultivation needs.

There is a very good reason for a plant to produce a swollen storage organ, and that is to help it overcome some period of adverse conditions, such as drought or cold, or both, but the first is the most important. Naturally enough, the same plant requires water at certain times of year to make it burst into life, flower and seed before the next adverse period.

WINTER RAINFALL

The Mediterranean type of climate provides just such a regime, with long, rather hot, dry summers followed by cool, moist winters, and it is especially in this type of environment that bulbous plants have evolved in their thousands, in several different plant families and in different ways, with tubers, corms, bulbs or rhizomes. Whatever the system adopted the overall effect is the same: the 'bulb' can lie in wait through the heat of the summer, full of stored energy, and often with buds ready formed, waiting for the falling temperatures and rising humidity of autumn. At the onset of the growing season most bulbs begin their activity by making new roots, the key to absorbing moisture and nutrients for the period of growth, which in turn leads to new storage material to overcome the next adverse dry spell. Above ground in the autumn things may or may not happen, depending upon the particular path of evolution, for some bulbs produce flowers straight away, often without leaves, giving us a group of extremely useful autumnal garden plants such as the autumn crocus, colchicum, sternbergia, nerines and belladonna lilies. Others react differently, and stay below ground for the winter months, though there has usually been plenty of root growth. Once the cold weather is over growth is rapid, and bulbs of this type have presented us with a mass of well-known early spring subjects such as daffodils, tulips, scillas, crocus and snowdrops. In both cases, whether autumn- or spring-flowering, the overall effect is the same: the plant makes its growth, flowers and fruits all during the period when there is moisture available, and by the time early summer has arrived the visible growth cycle is complete. Bulbs, and the resulting seeds, then lie in the soil through the inhospitable hot, dry period until the next autumn ready to begin a new growth season or, in the case of seeds, to germinate. It is a very efficient way for a perennial plant to cope with this climatic problem. Other plants have dealt with it in other ways, for example

Opposite:
Leucojum aestivum

Flowering Bulbs for the Garden

by being annual or ephemeral in duration, growing, seeding and dying all in the space of a few months while water is available.

I have mentioned the Mediterranean type of climate, but it would be wrong to think that this refers solely to the area bordering the Mediterranean Sea. There are many bulbous plants in this region, it is true, but the climate of winter rain and summer drought extends eastwards through Turkey and the Middle East as far as Soviet Central Asia, Afghanistan and the western Himalaya, and throughout this vast territory there is a wealth of bulbous plants, for example nearly a hundred different crocus species and about the same number of tulips and irises, and numerous others. Interestingly, if we follow roughly the same zone of latitude across the world to the Americas we find that some of the western states, especially California, also have this type of climate, and here too there are many bulbous plants that make very striking garden-worthy subjects, such as the dog's-tooth violets. Switching to the southern hemisphere produces another interesting link, for in South Africa at roughly the same zone of latitude there is again a host of bulbous plants, perhaps even more species than in the northern hemisphere. The 'Mediterranean-type' winter-rainfall area in South Africa is confined to the South West Cape region, and here bulbs abound in a

Opposite:
Tulipa fosteriana growing wild in Central Asia, flowering in spring prior to its long, dry dormant period

Left:
Erythronium 'White Beauty' is one of the excellent bulbs from the winter rainfall area of the western United States

bewildering array of colour, shape and form. Unfortunately for those of us who garden in northern Europe these species are mostly not quite hardy, and it is only in mild areas such as south-western Britain and southern Europe that they will flourish without protection. They do, however, make admirable subjects for an unheated or frost-free greenhouse. If we trace the same latitude zone across from South Africa to western South America we come to the Chilean Andes, and here again is a region of winter rains, with bulbous plants such as the gorgeous Chilean blue crocus (*Tecophilaea*), and many others which are mostly poorly known in European horticulture. Bringing these plants from the southern hemisphere into the north presents no great problems in cultivation for they merely alter their growth cycle by six months and continue to behave as winter growers. The Cape *Amaryllis belladonna*, for example, is most at home in our gardens in a hot situation where it can lie dormant through the summer, burst into flower in September or October and then make its new leaf growth during our winter and spring. Similarly, *Tecophilaea* from Chile fits into the same growth cycle as the European spring-flowering crocuses.

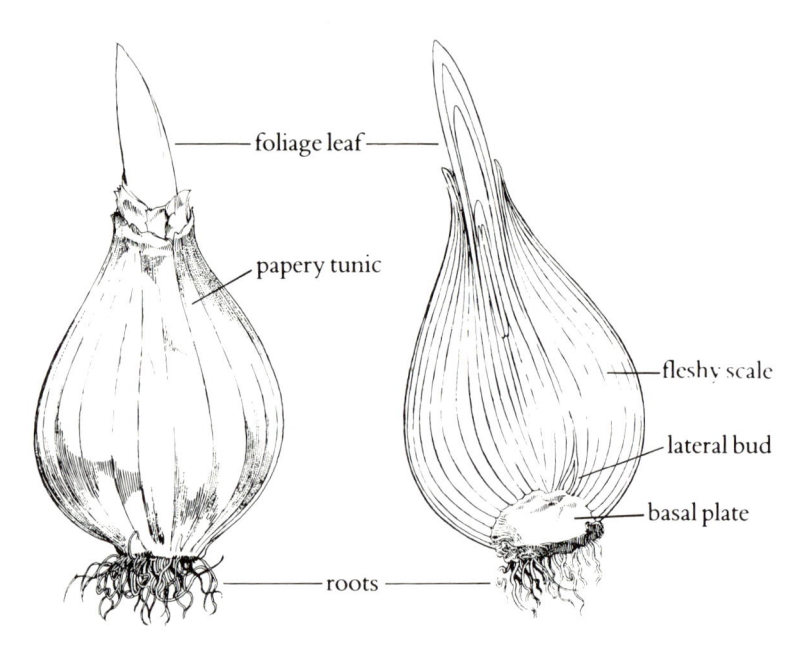

A true bulb showing papery tunics and, in section, the fleshy scales attached to the solid basal plate

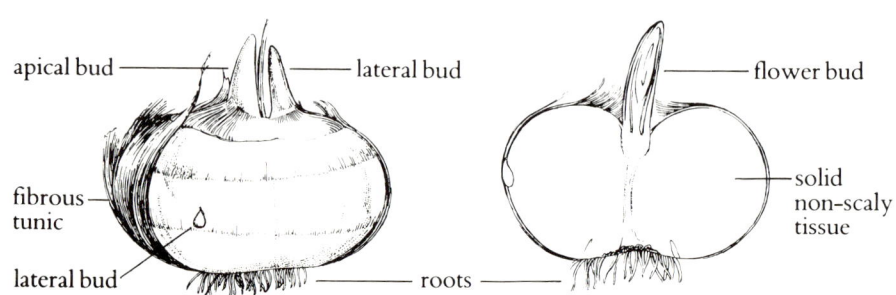

A corm showing tunics and apical and lateral buds. The cross section shows the solid non-scaly tissue

Summer rainfall

There are other regions in which the winter is rather dry (though in certain mountain areas there may be snow cover) and the summer is wet. Here too there are bulbous plants, this time with an underground storage organ to survive the cooler, dry winter period. From the garden viewpoint there are three important areas to be considered, the Eastern Cape of South Africa, Mexico, and eastern Asia. The first of these is noteworthy in that it provides the *Gladiolus* species, which have been painstakingly hybridized and selected to give us the many colourful cultivars available today. They are grown as summer-flowering bulbs and are lifted in winter to be stored away in the dry state, quite the reverse of the winter-growing crocuses, snowdrops, narcissus, tulips, etc. The Eastern Cape has many more, some hardy enough in many northern gardens to be left permanently in the open ground, such as *Eucomis*, *Galtonia*, *Rhodohypoxis*, *Dierama* and *Nerine bowdenii*.

The second area, Mexico, contains a great many bulbs, but few are hardy in northern Europe so we are mostly considering species which are lifted for the winter and planted out in spring. *Tigridia pavonia* is probably the most striking example but there is also the tuberose (*Polianthes tuberosa*) and *Calochortus barbatus*, which can be grown outside in mild areas.

The third area includes the Himalaya, China and Japan and, although this does not have such a great number and diversity of species as the Mediterranean winter-rainfall areas, it is important for a few genera, the most noteworthy of which is *Lilium*. This region gives us the marvellous Asiatic trumpet lilies, which have been hybridized to provide our gardens with some of the most striking summer-flowering bulbs of all. Rather more specialized in their needs are the related and equally gorgeous *Nomocharis*, which are more suited to the cooler, more moist climate of Scotland.

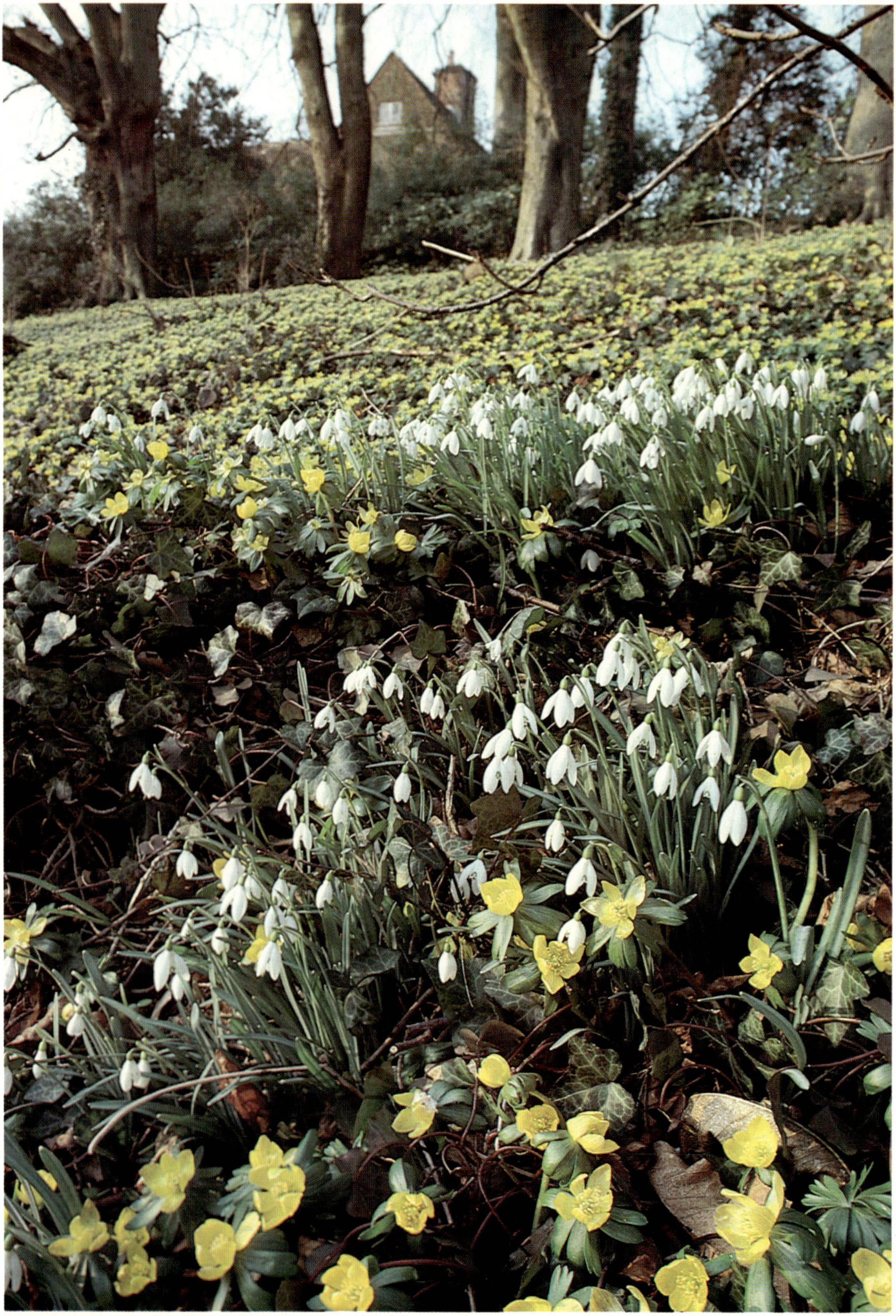

3
The Principles of Bulb Growing

Having reviewed the conditions to which bulbs in the wild are subjected, we now have to consider what can be done to simulate these in our gardens, for it stands to reason that we must, for the most part, provide a roughly similar pattern of growth and rest periods and temperature if the bulbs are to flourish. It is true that some bulbs are very tolerant of a wide range of situations, and daffodils are a good example here, thriving in many places, but others are very intolerant and we have to be fairly precise if the garden situation is going to be a home from home! First we will look at the general principles involved and then move on to greater detail of the different environments we can provide in a garden.

Winter-growing bulbs

Most of northern Europe and Britain has a climate which provides rain throughout the year, though because of higher temperatures in summer there is greater evaporation and the soil dries out more frequently. For winter-growing bulbs there is therefore no difficulty in getting enough moisture for the growth period, but there might be too much moisture in summer, when the resting bulbs need to be warm and relatively dry. Some species accept these conditions and thrive in ordinary garden soil, such as snowdrops, grape hyacinths, daffodils and star of Bethlehem, and their bulbs can be left in the ground all the time. A few even demand that they are not dried off in summer, such as the dog's-tooth violets. Others only survive from year to year if they receive a dryish rest period, and the most obvious way to provide this is to lift the bulbs after their leaves have withered away in late spring or early summer and to keep them in a dry place until the autumn; this is of course the time that nurserymen harvest and market their winter-growing bulbs. However, it is time-consuming and inconvenient for most of us to dig up our bulbs and replant them every year, and it is much better if we can improve the growing conditions enough to make permanent siting possible, the main aim usually being to provide soil which is relatively dry and warm in which the resting bulbs can ripen and form flower buds for the next season.

Warmth is obviously provided by the sun, so siting in an unshaded situation, perhaps with the protection of a fence, wall or evergreens on the north or north-east side to minimize the effect of cooling winds, will go a long way towards providing the right conditions.

Removal of excess summer rain can largely be achieved by good drainage, and heavy soils must be improved by the addition of sharp gritty sand, or, in really bad cases, even a system of land drains. The main aim is to lighten the soil so that the rain runs away from the dormant bulbs quickly instead of lying around them keeping them wet and cold. There are several ways in which this can be done, depending on the aspect of the garden and on personal preference.

Opposite:
Snowdrops and winter aconites naturalized in a semi-wooded situation

With a sloping garden the run-off of water should be sufficient to allow drying out in summer, but the slope should face south or south-west if it is to provide warm, sunny conditions. Such slopes can be terraced into raised beds, which can be a most attractive garden feature, and if the soil in these beds is composed of freely draining materials with plenty of gritty sand it will provide ideal conditions for many bulbs, and also for rock plants. Similarly, in level areas, raised beds can be constructed and filled with a well-drained medium to overcome any drainage problems with the natural soil. Rock gardens are a more attractive way of raising the growing area above the surrounding soil, and have the advantage that pockets can be built facing in almost any direction, giving a great variety of habitats.

For 'difficult' species requiring rather precise growing conditions we may resort to growing bulbs in pots in a frame or alpine house, where soil conditions are under direct control and water can be withheld at exactly the right time; some species are ideal for growing in containers on a terrace or patio, and in addition can look particularly effective.

Another way of removing excess moisture from around the dormant bulbs is to provide competition from other plants which are in active growth in summer, and thus use up moisture. Deciduous trees and shrubs are ideal, as they are leafless in the winter and early spring and allow plenty of light through to the bulbous plants while the latter are growing. However, care must be taken that the site is not too overgrown in summer or the resting bulbs will not receive enough warmth from the sun to ripen them and encourage the formation of flower buds. Planting bulbs on the sunny side of shrubs or trees provides a good spot for the bulbs and will brighten up the area when the shrubs are at their most dull. One should bear in mind, however, that competition for moisture also means competition for nutrients, so it will probably be necessary to feed bulbs in these situations in order to maintain vigour. (Further details will be given on page 32, under the individual methods of cultivation.)

Summer-growing bulbs

A rather different set of principles applies when dealing with summer bulbs, which are dormant in winter. In Europe our winters are often cold and damp, when ideally the resting bulbs should be dryish. The answer here is to improve the soil, if necessary, so that it drains freely and does not lie in a saturated state in winter. The soil may then drain so well that it becomes necessary to water the bulbs frequently during the summer growing period to prevent their drying out too much. An alternative method of cultivation is to dig up the bulbs in autumn at the end of the growing season, and to keep them stored away in a frost-free, dryish state, such as we do with gladiolus cultivars. Container cultivation is also very satisfactory, as the containers can be moved under cover for the winter and dried off to some extent. Lilies are particularly successful when treated in this way, as most species dislike their bulbs being cold and wet in winter and may well rot off. The main point to remember with summer bulbs is that plenty of moisture must be available while they are growing; in the hotter weather at this time of year this needs to be carefully attended to if proper growth is to be maintained, especially when the bulbs are container-grown.

Opposite:
Narcissus hybrids

The Principles of Bulb Growing

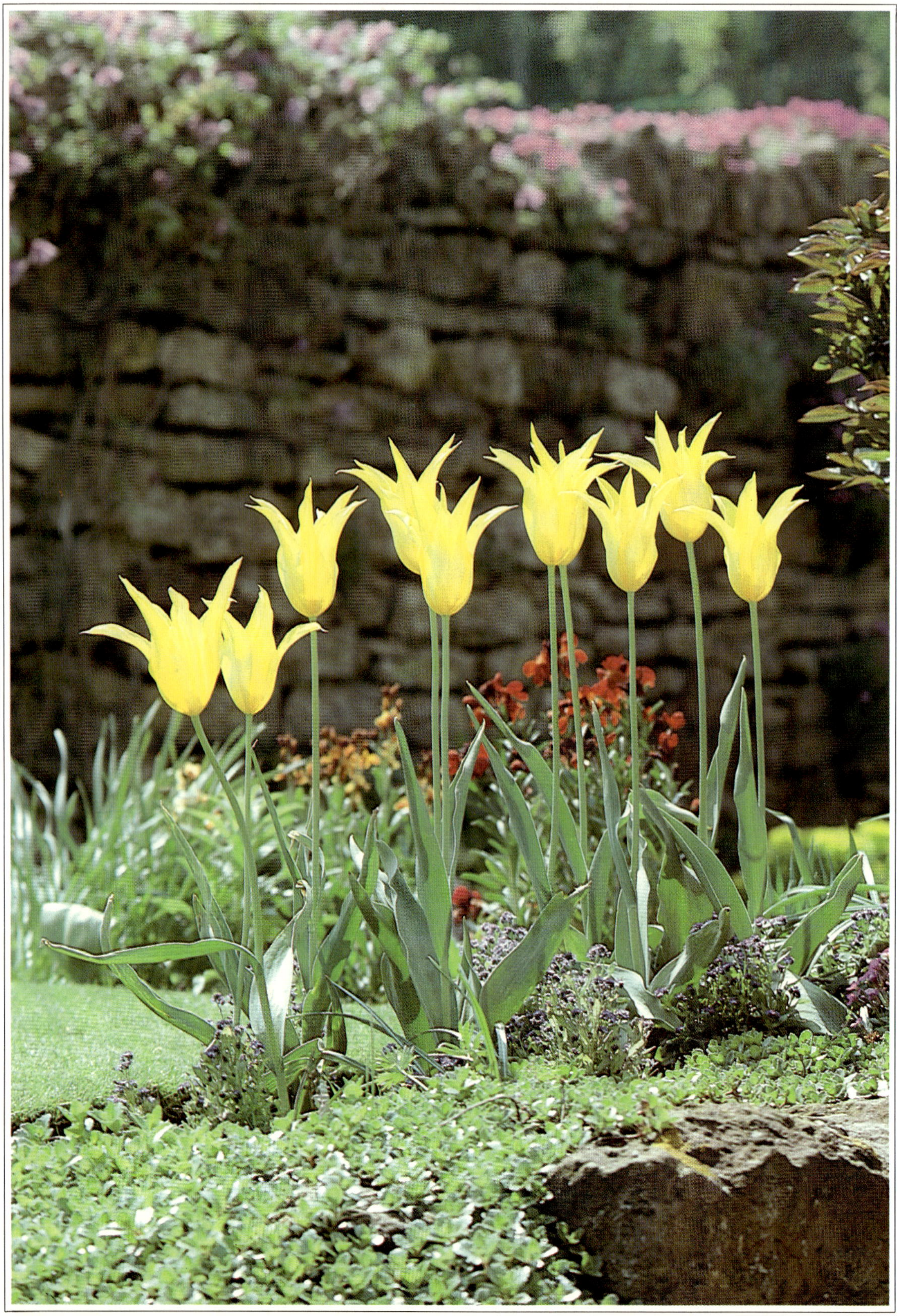

4
Flowering Bulbs around the Garden

Almost every garden has a range of different aspects that can be used for various types of plant; if not, a little planning and planting can soon provide some different habitats. Whether you are starting a brand-new garden on previously uncultivated soil or taking over an existing one, bulbs are of immense value in that their display can take effect within a few months of planting while the longer-term backbone of perennials, shrubs and trees is being built up. Let us look at the main types of environment we can provide, starting with those where bulbs might naturalize, and moving on through more elaborate situations such as rock gardens and raised beds to pot cultivation. The specialist treatment of the more unusual species in frames or unheated greenhouses is considered separately in the next chapter.

Naturalizing bulbs in grass

This can be a delightful method of growing bulbs which do not object to the competition from the grass, but before setting aside a section of the garden for this purpose there are a few points to consider. First, and most important, you must be prepared to leave the grass unmown for at least six weeks after the last bulbs have flowered. During this time the leaves will have matured and built up the strength of the bulb enough to carry it through the next season in sufficient health to flower again. It has been proved by practical experiments that mowing off the leaves of daffodils while they are still green weakens the bulbs and may eventually kill them off, and this also applies to other bulbous plants, as they all rely on their leaves to manufacture food for the bulbs. Most people like to cut the grass in summer, so that it not only looks tidy but is prevented from seeding about in the rest of the garden, so the choice of bulbs for planting in grass is clearly limited to those that grow and flower in autumn or spring, i.e. the 'winter growers'; summer bulbs would just get in the way. However, the choice is a wide one and there are plenty of species which come into growth after the mowing is finished in early autumn and before it is started in early summer. If the garden has a lawn in which you want to plant bulbs it is quite a good idea to keep one or two informally shaped sections for the bulbs so that you can mow around them, thus providing short grass for walking on between the groups of bulbs. As soon as the bulbs are ready to be cut down the whole area can be mown, though for the first cutting of the long grass shears or a grass hook may have to be used.

Planting in grass does not present any great problems, though it is obviously slightly more tedious than planting in an open border as there is the turf to contend with. There are two ways of dealing with this. Either a special bulb planter or a trowel can be used, to take out a core of turf and soil which is replaced after the bulb has been planted, or a more natural effect can be achieved by cutting out areas of turf with a spade, breaking up the soil and planting several bulbs and then fitting the turf back into place. If the soil is heavy and requires

Opposite: The graceful lily-flowered tulips such as 'West Point' are excellent in small groups among low-growing subjects

A bulb planter provides an easy method of planting in grass

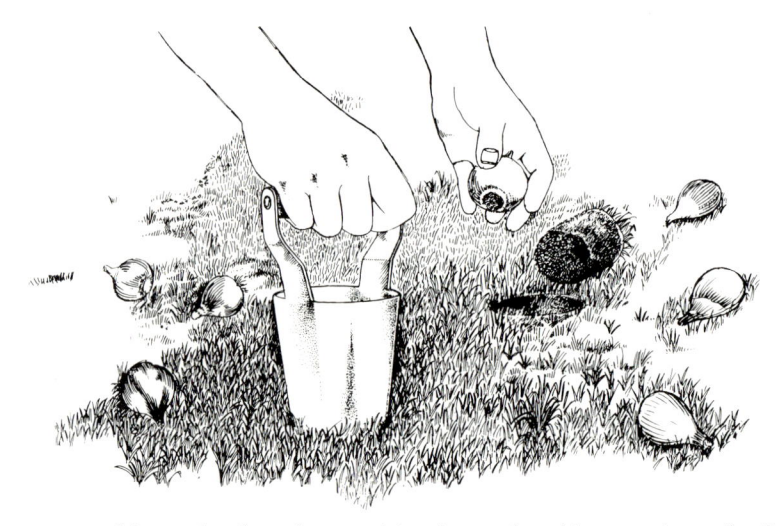

improvement this can be done by working in sand and humus (peat, leafmould) before planting the bulbs and replacing the turf. For the best effect these patches of bulbs should be irregularly arranged, as if they have arisen naturally. If they settle in well and begin to increase by division and seed of their own accord the informal effect is enhanced. Spacing for the smaller bulbs (e.g. grape hyacinths) should be 2.5–5 cm (1–2 in) apart, and for the more robust varieties (e.g. daffodils) 5–10 cm (2–4 in). Planting depths, too, depend roughly on size and vigour: as a general rule 5–6 cm (2–2½ in) of soil should be allowed above the top of the bulb for the smaller species, while for the bigger bulbs 10–12 cm (4–5 in) is recommended.

In general it is unnecessary to feed bulbs in grass, but if the soil is very poor and there are signs of deterioration in vigour then it may be necessary to use a general fertilizer. You must bear in mind, however, that any nourishment intended for the bulbs is going to increase the vigour of the grass as well, which will in turn compete more strongly with the bulbs. A fertilizer which does not contain too much nitrogen is to be preferred, as this would result in much leaf growth, and a dressing of sulphate of potash or a potash-rich proprietary brand of general fertilizer is best, as potash does encourage the formation of healthy, free-flowering bulbs, whatever the situation in which they are grown, and healthy bulbs will be better able to stand the competition.

The most suitable site for naturalizing bulbs in grass is to some extent dictated by the needs of the grass itself, for it will only grow really well in a fairly open situation, which suits the bulbs too. Sloping areas are satisfactory as drainage tends to be better, and the overall appearance on such sites is rather pleasant with subjects such as daffodils and crocus in the early spring. Small, meadow-like patches around fruit trees also provide plenty of scope for trying out various bulbs in grass, for these areas are not usually regarded as potential lawns and are thus less closely mown. A really finely maintained lawn is not a suitable place for growing bulbs, either practically or from the aesthetic viewpoint because they do not really fit in with the formal perfection of such a feature. Much more suitable is a piece of rough grass where other wild flowers can be allowed to develop, such as buttercups, the early-flowering British umbellifer *Anthriscus* and the blue borage *Pentaglottis sempervirens*, all of which I find capable of withstanding light mowing from about June onwards, when they have finished flowering, until September.

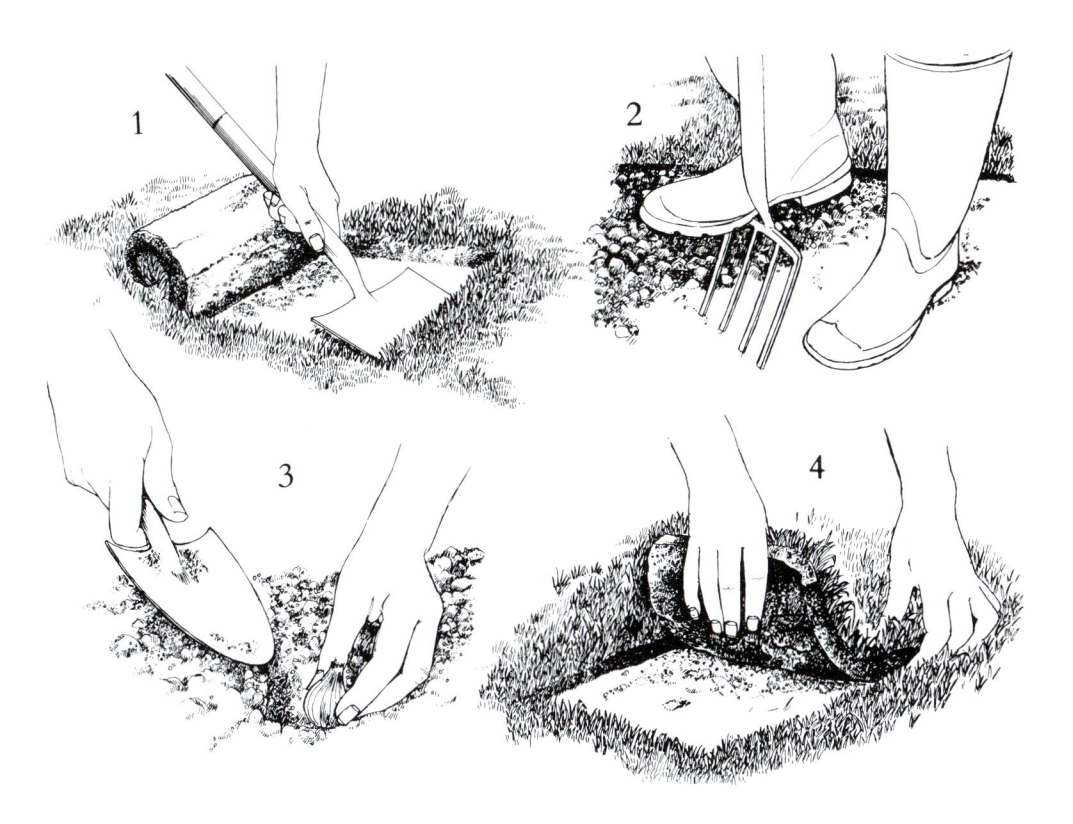

If autumn bulbs are planted, such as crocus and colchicum, mowing will have to cease in early September as the first ones begin to push through soon after this, but it is wise to continue cutting the grass as late as you possibly can so that it is not too long and vigorous again by the time the small spring bulbs appear; this can be a problem in mild winters when the grass barely stops growing. On the whole the choice of mower is unimportant, though on heavy soils a rotary or hover type is better than ones with rollers which tend to compact the turf much more.

The excessive use of selective weedkillers is best avoided on areas where bulbs are planted, and also any mechanical activities such as spiking which might damage bulbs near the surface.

If there is a space in the garden where a small patch of grass can be given over to naturalized bulbs it can provide a great deal of enjoyment through the autumn and winter months, and it is well worth experimenting by planting any odd spare bulbs which come your way; occasionally there is a nice surprise when an unlikely subject settles in and thrives, such as the small unexpected patch of *Iris histrioides* which has built up in my own garden, where it looks much more natural in the grass than in a pot or weed-free border.

A list of bulbs worth trying in grass appears on page 116.

If groups of bulbs are to be planted in grass it is best to lift a whole strip of turf (1). Then fork over the soil (2), plant the bulbs (3), and replace the turf (4), firming gently

Bulbs in the shrub border

One of the noteworthy features of areas around trees and shrubs is that once the initial planting has taken place they are normally fairly uncultivated, and apart from weeding, which is usually a superficial activity, the ground is left undisturbed. This makes them ideal spots for growing certain bulbs which can be left to increase and colonize otherwise rather bare areas. As already mentioned, deciduous trees or shrubs are best as they cast only slight shade and use up little moisture when the bulbs are growing in the early part of the year, and they then remove excess soil water in summer when they are in leaf and the bulbs are dormant.

Within this heading there are two possible planting areas, the first actually in shade under the canopy of the woody plants and the second in the dappled shade or full sun between shrubs. To illustrate this point we can pick out plants that prefer one or other of these sites: for example, snowdrops and dog's-tooth violets enjoy the cool, shadier areas, while daffodils need the extra light to flourish.

One point to bear in mind is that trees and shrubs generally use up most of the nutrients in the soil, and it is usually necessary to feed bulbs if vigour is to be maintained. Slow release (pelleted) fertilizers are ideal for this, keeping to those

Camassia leichtlinii is a tallish bulb suitable for grouping in a border. This is the double white form

which have a low nitrogen content; the proportions of N (nitrogen), P (phosphate) and K (potassium) are shown on the packets of proprietary brands and can be compared before deciding which to buy. Bonemeal is also suitable. Whatever is used, it should be given as a light dressing in early autumn or early spring before the bulbs emerge.

Before planting, which takes place in late summer to autumn when the bulbs arrive in the shops and nurseries, it is best to break up the soil and incorporate old, well-decayed compost, leafmould or peat, taking care not to cut too many roots, though most trees will suffer no harm if a few are damaged. Once the bulbs are established no further cultivation should be necessary, except for weeding, but it is beneficial to give an annual top-dressing in autumn of humus in the form of compost or leafmould; avoid manure unless it is really old and crumbly, when a lot of the nitrogen will have been washed out. This will benefit both the bulbs and the shrubs, and provides a pleasing dark background for the flowering bulbs. If autumn-flowering species are included in the planting, the top-dressing will obviously have to be timed to avoid these.

Areas under and around trees and shrubs are normally informal and the planting should be aimed at providing a semi-natural effect with irregular drifts of bulbs rather than formal clumps. In time, subjects such as snowdrops, chionodoxa and star of Bethlehem will increase and spread around by themselves and add to the natural effect, but daffodil varieties usually stay in compact clumps so that the initial layout is important. To do this, either make a rough sketch of the positions of the main trees and shrubs and plan on paper which bulbs will give the best effect and then purchase them, or first buy the bulb varieties you particularly want and then decide where they will look best. You might, for

Galanthus caucasicus is a suitable subject for naturalizing at the front of a shrub border

example, have a winter-flowering *Viburnum farreri* (*fragrans*) and decide to make a real splash of winter colour by adding an underplanting of purple-pink *Cyclamen coum*; or you may, conversely, argue that it is better to spread the interest around the garden and plant *Cyclamen coum* near a summer-flowering shrub which is dull in winter and a spring-flowering bulb near the viburnum to provide colour when it has finished flowering. It is really a matter of personal preference.

For areas under and around trees and shrubs the most suitable bulbs are mainly autumn to spring flowering; that is, they belong to the 'winter rainfall' group and are dormant in summer. There are a few summer growers that are useful for these situations, and the most important ones in this category are the lilies, which mostly enjoy cool, dappled shade from surrounding shrubs rather than full sun, especially in the warmer, drier parts of the country. These will not thrive, however, if there is too much competition from the roots of other plants and it will be necessary to prepare the planting area well, with plenty of decayed organic matter dug in deeply. In dry summers especially it will be necessary to water frequently, as the woody plants will be using up a lot of the available moisture and, because many lilies produce feeding roots from the stem just near the soil surface, it is also beneficial to give them a top-dressing of leafmould, old compost or peat while in growth. As long as vigour is maintained they can be left from year to year, but as soon as there is any sign of deterioration they should be dug up in early autumn, and the site prepared as before and then replanted. Careful siting of lilies is also needed if the best effect is to be obtained. They are ideal, for example, for planting amid rhododendrons which have long finished their flowering period and in summer provide a deep green background for the brightly coloured lilies. Some of the orange colours, such as that of the tiger lily, can make a surprisingly attractive combination with purplish-leaved shrubs such as *Cotinus coggygria* 'Royal Purple', while the yellow trumpet lilies can be associated successfully with variegated-leaved plants.

The North American camassias are also summer flowering; they enjoy moist situations so are suitable for a cool position between shrubs, which will provide some shade. Although a few species and varieties are fairly easy to obtain from bulb nurseries they are seldom seen in gardens and can add a touch of the unusual to the shrub border, but plant them near something which is out of flower in summer for they are not colourful enough to compete with other, more showy subjects.

A list of bulbs suitable for shrub borders and under trees appears on page 116.

Bulbs and herbaceous perennials

In contrast to the garden features previously mentioned, herbaceous borders are usually intensively cultivated areas, as a lot of the plants in them require frequent lifting and splitting up to maintain their vigour, and they also need a relatively rich soil so the border must be dug over and enriched from time to time. None of these activities suits the type of bulbs that prefer undisturbed conditions where they can settle in and increase over a period of years, so subjects such as crocus, snowdrops and cyclamen are quite out of place in the traditional herbaceous border. Some of the more robust, taller bulbs can, however, be satisfactorily incorporated into such a scheme, either as permanent plantings or for filling gaps for the summer months. In the latter case half-hardy bulbs, which in most parts of the country have to be lifted for the winter, are suitable, such as *Tigridia pavonia*, *Gladiolus* and *Galtonia*.

Permanent groups of bulbs are best marked in some way so that they can be avoided when dormant in summer, and a small cane will do, or a chart can be made showing the positions of the various plants. Groups of daffodils and tulips in different varieties are very useful, as they are strong growers and flower at a time when there is little else in the herbaceous border and, if the soil is well-supplied with moisture, which it should be if such plants as michaelmas daisies are going to thrive, the summer snowflake (*Leucojum aestivum*) is also a suitable subject. In sunny, well-drained positions there is no better and more stately border plant than the crown imperial (*Fritillaria imperialis*) in yellow or red forms, and for similar situations there are the tall drumstick *Allium* species such as *A. aflatunense*, the bulbous English, Spanish and Dutch irises and the hardy, bright reddish-purple *Gladiolus byzantinus*. These are all early summer flowering and help to spread the season of interest in the border, which is essentially a high-summer feature of the garden.

However, there are also bulbs which will assist in the mid- to late-summer display, and lilies are the prime example, for their flowers are showy enough to compete with all the brightly coloured herbaceous plants. Even so, it pays to place small groups of lilies near some shorter plants with fairly neutral colours, such as greyish foliage or white flowers, in order to accentuate their beauty rather than compete with it. Lilies require special treatment and, unlike daffodils which can be left alone for many years, will probably need to be lifted every other year or so in the autumn in order to re-make the site (see lilies on page 86). Many of the modern lily hybrids are strong growers requiring deep, rich soil, and are therefore ideally suited to the perennial border. *Crinum × powellii* in its pink and white forms also has a place here, and as they are tall plants they can go towards the back, using some shorter subjects in front to hide the somewhat unattractive leaves of the crinum. These have enormous bulbs which, as long as they go on flowering, are best left undisturbed for years. Montbretia, too, is an ideal border plant, nowadays available in various colourful cultivars, and its taller, rather stately relatives *Curtonus* and *Crocosmia masonorum* are also well worth growing.

With all bulbs planted in the herbaceous border it is essential to know where they are when dormant; when digging a hole to plant something new in the autumn, winter or spring it is very annoying to find that you are spearing bulbs already in residence. Another point to watch is that after the spring-flowering bulbs have died down their sites do not become densely overgrown with other plants which will keep them cool and shady, thus preventing them from forming buds for the next year.

'Filler' bulbs for the herbaceous border use up the available gaps during the summer months, and these areas should also be large enough not to become overgrown by surrounding plants. Planting of these gaps is carried out in spring, usually when the danger of any serious frosts is past as most of these plants are tender. The sites can be prepared individually before planting, but for most of the bulbs recommended for this purpose a well-drained, fairly rich soil is best. At the front of borders the colourful varieties of *Anemone coronaria*, 'De Caen' and 'St Brigid', are ideal and, although perennial and hardy, are better replaced each year, for they deteriorate in all but the very mildest of gardens. There is plenty of choice of taller bulbs for farther back in the border, the most obvious example being gladiolus, available in a wide range of colours and types. For something slightly more unusual than the cultivars, *Gladiolus callianthus* (*Acidanthera bicolor*), with its long-tubed, scented white flowers in late summer, is well worth growing, as are the amazing tigridias. These have large, brightly-coloured, short-lived flowers in succession, so it is best to plant about fifteen to twenty bulbs at least so that there are a few blooms opening each day. *Galtonia candicans* is a tall, white-flowered Cape bulb, again late summer flowering, which stands out best if planted in a group in front of some darkish foliage where the shape of the pendent, bell-like flowers can be seen clearly.

In autumn, before the onset of any sharp frosts, when their foliage is dying down, these tender bulbs can be lifted for the winter, dried out a little and then stored in a cool but frost-free shed, garage or greenhouse in some loose peat which should not be dust dry, or on the other hand too soggy, but with just enough moisture present to prevent the bulbs from shrivelling. In spring they can be removed just before planting out into the garden, cleaned of any old soil and loose bulb coats and treated with a fungicide if there is any sign of damage; the systemic fungicides based on benomyl are satisfactory for this purpose.

A selection of bulbs suitable for planting in the herbaceous border appears on page 115.

Opposite:
Some of the larger *Narcissus* varieties in a spring border display

Below:
The modern *Crocosmia* hybrids make excellent and stately border plants

Flowering Bulbs around the Garden

Bulbs for rock gardens and raised beds

A rock garden can provide a whole range of different aspects – sunny and shady, dry and damp – to suit a variety of plants. The majority of bulbs prefer good drainage, and this is automatically provided because the pockets of a rock garden are built up above the surrounding ground and can be filled with a gritty soil mixture during the construction process. The rock garden is sometimes built into the slope of a convenient bank, and here again the drainage is likely to be naturally good. Raised beds present a similar but simpler method of achieving good drainage on heavy soils, and if raised considerably above the natural ground level can make the viewing and maintenance of a collection of smaller bulbs easier. The main difference between rock gardens and raised beds is that the former are informal in design and intended to look as natural as possible, whereas raised beds are usually square or rectangular, though there is no reason why they should not be round or irregularly shaped. The surface of the raised bed will, however, be more or less flat, with only one aspect, open to the sun, whereas the rock garden has different levels with some pockets representing south-facing sun traps while others might be north-facing and cool, with a wide variety of possible intermediates as well, depending upon the wishes of the constructor.

By definition the rock garden is constructed of some type of rock. As far as the plants are concerned the choice of rock is relatively unimportant; it is more a matter of personal preference. Some people may prefer the greyish, irregular shapes provided by waterworn limestone, while others choose the more angular, brownish blocks of sandstone. There are many other types as well, and availability and price will also have a great bearing upon which is chosen. There are also manufactured 'rocks' available now, some of them hollow inside to make them light for ease of working, and these are also suitable for the 'bones' of a rock garden, however objectionable they may be to the purist!

Raised beds, on the other hand, are not restricted to rock for their construction, though this is of course an attractive medium to use. Any manufactured reconstructed stone, concrete blocks, bricks or even railway sleepers can be used. The beds can be any height up to about 60 cm (24 in); any higher than this can cause problems with over-drying in summer, though it does not matter if only summer-dormant bulbs are planted. The raised bed can be filled as building progresses, with a layer of brick rubble or other such coarse

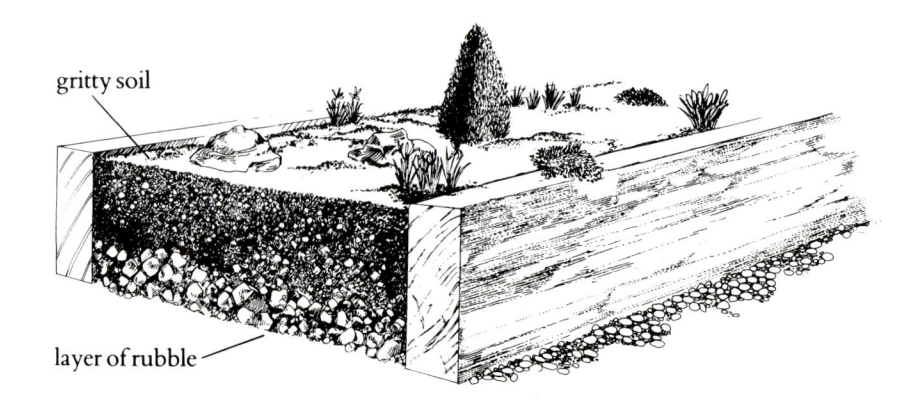

A simple raised bed providing the extra drainage which many small bulbs enjoy

drainage material followed by a gritty soil mixture which will drain freely. The same applies to the pockets on a rock garden, which should have a layer of drainage material in the bottom topped up with a similarly well-drained soil mix made up of, very approximately, three parts by volume of loam, one part very coarse gritty sand or fine shingle and one part moss peat (not the black bog peat). If ready-mixed compost is more convenient to buy than the separate ingredients then a John Innes No. 2 is best, to which you can add extra drainage material in the proportion of three compost to one coarse sand or shingle. For the first year it is unnecessary to feed the bulbs in the rock garden or raised bed, but after this it is advisable to scatter a light dressing of a granulated fertilizer which is high in potash. Any commercial product which has nitrogen/phosphate/potassium (NPK) proportions of about 15:15:30 will be suitable, and this should be applied in early autumn or early spring before the main push of growth begins. However, where rock plants are grown in association with bulbs care must be taken not to overfeed, as they may be forced out of character by a rich diet; for example, compact cushion plants may become loose and unattractive. It is better in these circumstances to err on the side of undernourishment and give only very light dressings of fertilizer, or none at all if the bulbs and alpines are all growing satisfactorily.

Rock gardens normally contain a mixture of suitable plants, of which bulbs form an essential part, whereas raised beds can be restricted to bulbous plants, though they do become a much more attractive feature if rock plants are included. Any plant which likes open, sunny situations in well-drained soil is suitable and, in the case of beds built with drystone walls (i.e. without cement), there is the extra possibility of putting suitable wall plants in the crevices.

For both rock gardens and raised beds the bulbous plants we are most likely to use are those that flower between autumn and spring, which liven up the early and late parts of the year and then die down for the summer, leaving the colourful rock plants to fill that season. Most summer-flowering bulbs are robust, taller-growing plants which require plenty of moisture and are out of place in these situations, though there are a few exceptions, such as rhodohypoxis, and one or two lilies which are slender and graceful enough to be acceptable and in character. The extra drainage provided opens up a whole range of possibilities for the spring and autumn bulbs and, since the rock garden and raised bed is really gardening in miniature, it is possible to try many of the interesting small bulbs which would be rather lost in an open border among other plants. With separate soil pockets a rock garden also offers the possibility of mixing various composts for different plants and choosing the best aspect for each variety. Erythroniums (dog's-tooth violets) and snowdrops, for example, prefer a semi-shaded, cool position in humus-rich soil which does not sun-bake in summer, whereas sternbergia, *Iris reticulata*, many of the crocus and dwarf tulip species all require dry, sunny conditions while they are dormant.

Of all garden features a rock garden is probably one of the most versatile, as almost everything is under the control of the gardener, from the building to the planting and subsequent cultivation of the bulbs. As a great many bulbs are mountain plants anyway, they look in character and perform very satisfactorily in such a situation.

A list of bulbs suitable for rock gardens and raised beds appears on page 117.

Bulbs in window-boxes and other containers

The window-box has always been a popular method of growing plants, especially for people with a restricted area available for gardening. Other types of container are also going through a period of great popularity with the increased interest in the patio and terrace as a garden feature.

There are quite a number of bulbs which are suitable for planting in window-boxes for a spring display, and hyacinths, crocuses and dwarf tulips are of course prime examples. These are usually removed after flowering to make way for other plants for the summer, so their long-term cultivation is of little concern. Almost any type of soil will suffice for these, provided that it is reasonably well-drained, since they are purchased with flowers already formed within the bulb and all they require is something to root into and provide moisture for the shoot to develop. Frost is also not normally too much of a problem, as a window-box tucked up against the house receives a certain amount of protection.

Bulbs grown in containers over a longer period, standing out in the open on a terrace, need more careful attention. There are fewer suitable ones, and summer-flowering subjects such as lilies are the most rewarding, though there is no reason why the town gardener with only a patio and no open garden space should not plant, for example, daffodils and tulips in tubs. For longer term planting a reasonable potting compost must be chosen, and for vigorous plants such as lilies I prefer a loam-based medium such as John Innes No. 3. The bottom of the container, over the holes, is covered with broken crocks, stones or gravel for drainage; then, if you can get it, some old, rotted, crumbly manure or one of the proprietary counterparts – a layer of about 5 cm (2 in) will do. Suitable containers will be at least 20 cm (8 in) deep and 20 cm (8 in) wide across the rim, so there will be room for a good layer of potting compost above and below the bulbs. Most bulbs need at least 5–10 cm (2–4 in) of soil above them; this is

Old stone sinks provide perfect conditions for both alpines and some of the smaller bulbs

―――――――――――――――――――――――――――――FLOWERING BULBS AROUND THE GARDEN

Eucomis comosa is a good late summer bulb for the terrace or patio

particularly true of a lot of the lilies, which have roots coming out of the stem above the bulb as well as from the base of the bulb itself. Potting up will either take place in the autumn, when most bulbs can be obtained, or in the spring for some of the summer-flowering subjects such as acidanthera, eucomis and galtonia; it depends on when they are on sale from the nurseries.

   Once planted in their containers they should be watered well to moisten the compost right through, but then only sparingly until there are signs of growth pushing through. The early stage, before rooting has begun, is when bulbs are most likely to rot off through overwatering. For those planted in the autumn, the winter is a tricky period. Heavy, prolonged frosts can freeze containers solid,

A wooden tub planted with bulbs showing the various layers of drainage and compost material

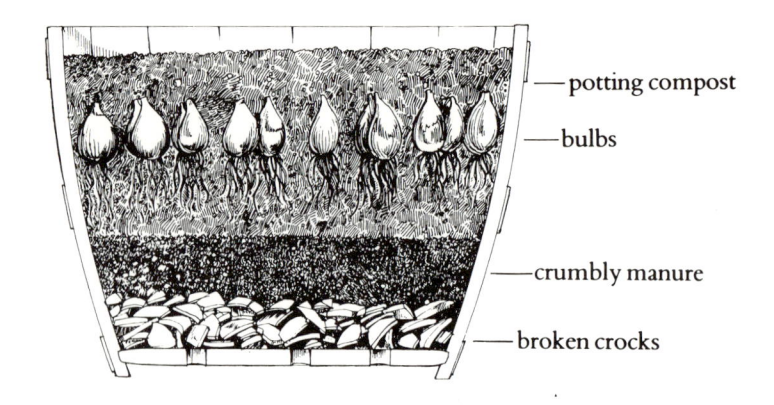

- potting compost
- bulbs
- crumbly manure
- broken crocks

possibly causing damage to the bulbs and sometimes cracking clay pots. With containers which are movable I prefer to keep these in a frost-free greenhouse or shed for the winter but there must be very little extra warmth or they will be forced into early growth. Another way is to plunge the pots up to their rims in the garden in sand, peat, or even the soil, just to prevent frost getting in from the sides as well as the top. People without facilities for this can alleviate the problem by grouping the containers together in the most sheltered part of the patio and draping old sacking, woollens or some other protective material around them during periods of severe frost. In spring, when the danger of frosts has passed, they can be spaced out to give them light and air until they reach their flowering time, when they can be moved about to wherever they are needed to achieve the best effect. Spring-potted bulbs are less of a problem as they can be left until the cold weather is over before being planted.

A useful tip concerning tall subjects such as lilies, which will need staking, is to place a short cane in the container at planting time, positioning it so that it does not spear the bulbs. Later on, when the stems are tall or need support, this cane can be replaced in the same hole by a long one. The danger of spearing a bulb is thus avoided without unsightly tall canes being present while there is nothing showing in the pots.

Obviously, tall vigorous bulbs like lilies, eucomis and acidanthera will require plenty of water while they are growing, and it should not be assumed in rainy weather that the soil in the pots is damp; sometimes the foliage shields the pot from the rain. It is better to soak the pots thoroughly every now and again rather than to give them a frequent quick spray over, and with lilies I am sure it is best to let them almost dry out before soaking again; certainly they should not be kept permanently soggy.

Feeding is equally necessary, as strong-growing bulbs will soon use up the available nutrients. A good general, well-balanced fertilizer is appropriate, and I prefer one of the granular slow-release ones which can be scattered on the surface and left to dissolve slowly as the plants are watered. Liquid fertilizers applied once a week are just as good if you are well organized and remember to feed regularly.

Repotting can take place between the autumn and early spring before the bulbs start to grow vigorously. It is a repeat of the original potting, the bulbs being cleaned of any old soil, dead roots and stems and repotted in the same way.

Potted bulbs plunged in a frame for protection from frost (left). Alternatively, large pots can be wrapped in sacking during winter (right)

The tender bulbs, which one would normally buy and pot up in spring, can either be stacked away dry in their pots in a frost-free place for the winter or they can be removed from their containers in autumn, cleaned and stored away, again in a frost-free place, ready for potting in spring.

The number of bulbs for a container depends very much upon the size and depth of the container, and on the species involved. Vigorous lilies, for example, need at least a 20 cm (8 in) diameter pot for each bulb, whereas the same sized pot would take several acidanthera corms or tulip bulbs. A 30 cm (12 in) container would take three bulbs of the smaller kinds of lily such as 'Connecticut King', and I find that with regular feeding several bulbs will grow successfully in quite small pots. I have, for example, good regular displays of four spikes of *Lilium regale* in a 25 cm (10 in) pot.

The choice of container is partly up to individual taste and is not too important. I prefer not to use plastic ones, which can stay very wet for a long time if the weather is dull and rainy. Earthenware ones look very attractive but can crack in frosty weather if they are not put away for protection. Wooden tubs are also very pleasant, but of course are not indestructible though they will last for at least five years, and probably more like ten, if they are looked after. The ornamental ones constructed from cement or glass fibre are tough and can look in place on a modern patio.

Propagation of bulbous plants

For most gardeners propagation of bulbous plants will be a matter of digging up established clumps during the resting period and dividing them into single bulbs, then replanting in the same way as the original stock. Nearly all bulbs are dealt with while they are dormant, usually in the late summer or early autumn.

Flowering Bulbs for the Garden

Flowering Bulbs around the Garden

Hardy bulbs such as daffodils and crocuses are replanted straight away, but tender ones such as gladiolus are cleaned and stored for the winter, and the offset bulbs removed for propagation purposes. A few bulbs are best lifted and divided in their growing season, for example winter aconites, snowdrops and snowflakes (*Leucojum*), and this is best done just after flowering; the bulbs are of course planted back immediately without drying them out.

Many bulbs will increase naturally like this, but some are reluctant to divide or produce offsets and it may be necessary to encourage them. There are various ways of doing this. Members of the Amaryllidaceae and Liliaceae with tight scaly bulbs and a basal plate, such as hyacinths, daffodils, scilla, etc., will form bulblets if an x-shaped cut is made in summer deep into the basal plate and scales; thin

Opposite:
Allium aflatunense, an excellent onion relative for the early summer

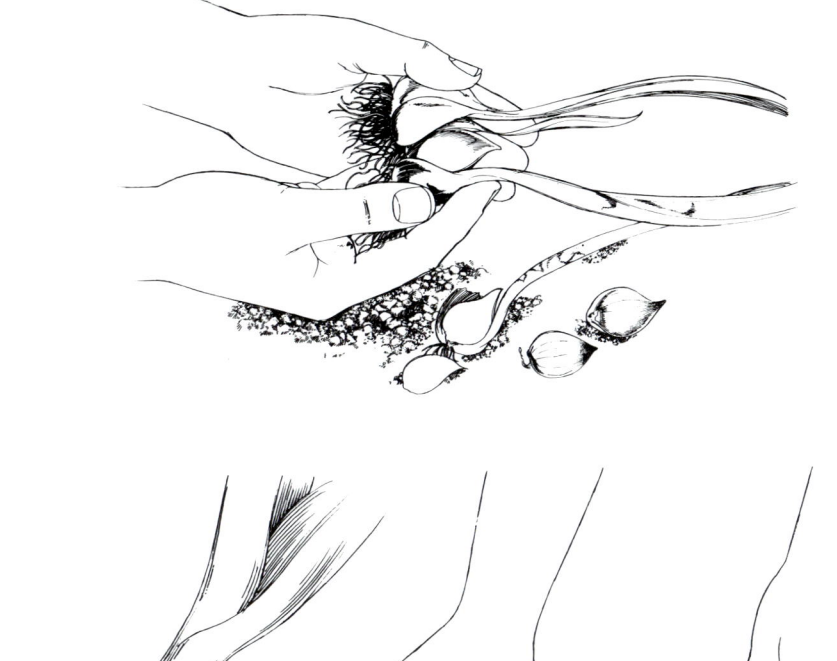

Bulbs which increase naturally can easily be divided, usually when dormant

Gladiolus cormlets are removed from the parent corm and grown separately until large enough to be used for display plantings

FLOWERING BULBS FOR THE GARDEN

pieces of broken clay pot are then inserted in the cuts to stop them growing back together. Young bulbs should form on the cut surfaces during the next growing season. Bulbs with loose scales, such as lilies, can be increased by removing a few scales from the outside of the bulbs, preferably in late summer or autumn when they are at the end of their growing period and due for repotting or replanting. These scales can be planted shallowly in boxes of a sand–peat mixture in a frame

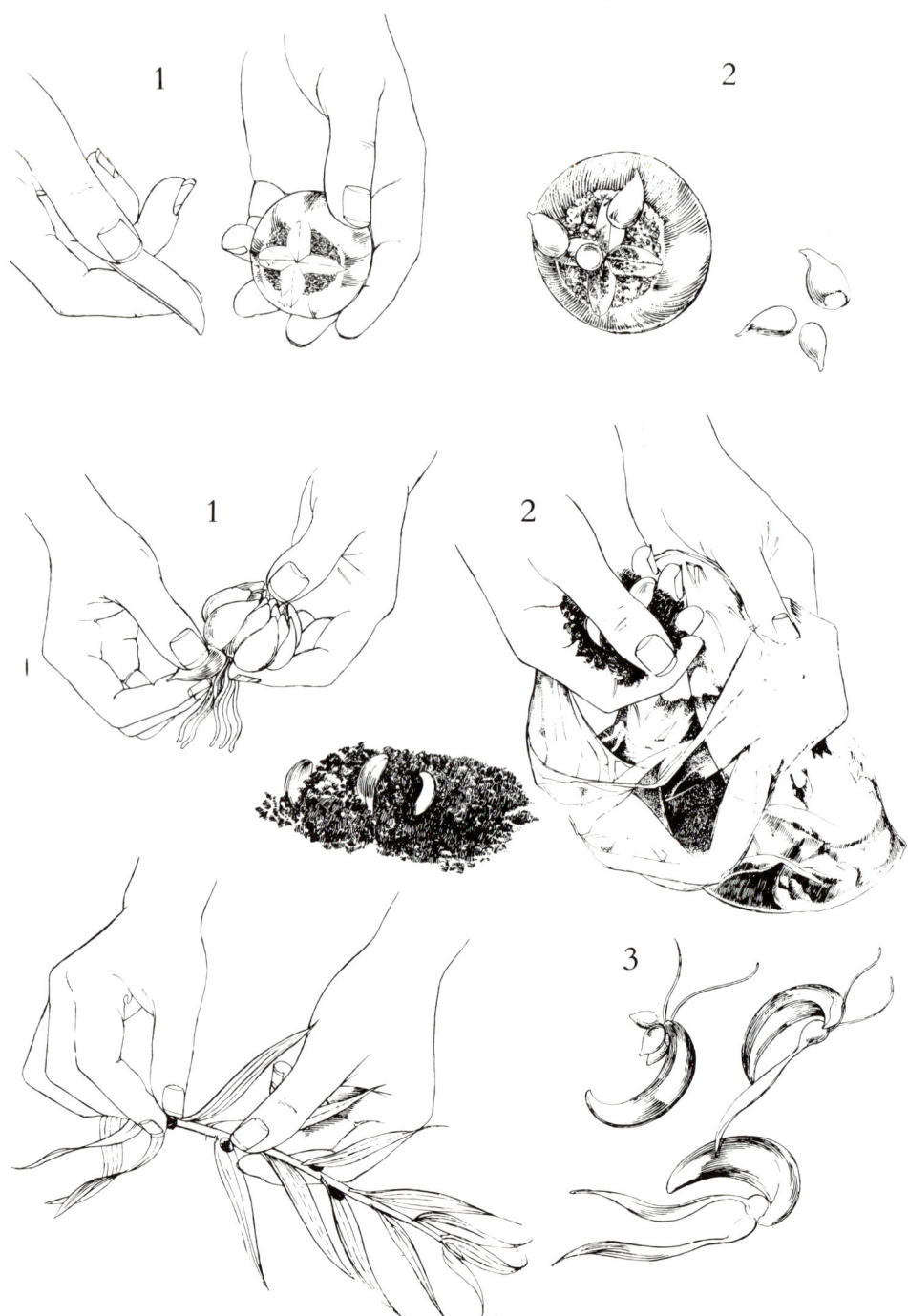

Scoring the basal plate (1), results in bulblets forming (2)

Removing scales from lily bulbs (1), placing them in a polythene bag with some moist peat (2), will result in small bulbils being formed (3)

Bulbils in leaf axils of lilies can be removed and potted up or greenhouse where they will form small bulblets, or they can be put into a polythene bag with some just moist moss peat or vermiculite and kept indoors until bulblets appear; the young bulblets can then be removed and potted up in compost. Some lilies produce bulbils on their stems, either just below ground level or in the axils of the leaves, and these too can be removed and potted up.

Young bulbs propagated in this way are all identical to their parents. The other major way of propagating them is by seed, when variation from the parents may occur, either by natural variation within the species (sometimes with mutations occurring, such as albinos) or by hybridization with a related species; the latter can be by chance or by deliberate action of the gardener. Any plants raised from seed by the gardener for his own use are likely to have an advantage over those bought in from elsewhere, as he is automatically encouraging those most suitable for his own climate and soil conditions; unsuitable ones will probably die before they reach maturity. The disadvantage is that bulbs from seed take at least three years to reach flowering size and some, like tulips, take up to seven years.

On the whole it is best to collect seeds and sow them either straight away or at the latest in the following autumn, but spring is best in the case of tender summer growers. A proprietary seed compost is suitable, with coarse grit scattered over the seeds after they have been thinly sown; either plastic or clay pots can be used, but clay pots require plunging up to the rim in sand to keep them uniformly moist and to stop them splitting in frosty weather. The best place for the pots is in a cold frame, where they will receive the cold treatment necessary for germination of most hardy bulbs; this also gives a little protection from very heavy rains which may knock the seeds out of the pots. Germination is likely to take place some time during the winter or spring (summer for the summer growers), but if nothing appears do not throw them away; some seeds can lie dormant for more than a year before germinating and some lilies have a delayed type of germination.

After germination the young seedlings should be kept growing for as long as possible by careful watering, and a very weak liquid feed will be beneficial at this time. When they die down the pots can be emptied and the young bulbs sorted out ready for repotting into larger pots in a richer compost, or into a bulb frame for growing on.

Some tender bulbs which are normally bought and planted out in the spring, such as tigridias, are better propagated by seeds sown in a slightly heated greenhouse in late winter to give a longer growing season.

There are many other methods of inducing bulbs to increase, and for those interested in this fascinating subject there are several specialist books on propagation available.

Pests and diseases

This unpleasant business should not cause too much concern among amateur gardeners with a mixture of bulbs around the garden, as they are by and large trouble-free. Many bulbous plants, flowering in winter or early spring and in the autumn, avoid the time when there are many pests, such as aphids and caterpillars, about; diseases, too, are much more prevalent during warm weather.

Flowering Bulbs for the Garden

A delightful spring display of daffodils, crown imperials, tulips, snowflakes, grape hyacinths and erythroniums. Well grown bulbs like these seldom suffer from pests and diseases in the garden

Pests are on the whole easier to deal with as they can be seen and despatched by some means before too much damage has resulted. Any physical damage to leaves can usually be tracked down to slugs, vine weevils, cutworms, caterpillars or lily beetles, and as some of these are active at night it may be necessary to go out with a torch to find them. Hand picking can account for quite a lot of these larger pests, though the squeamish may prefer to go to the local garden shop and buy one of the many powders or sprays; these are always provided with clear instructions about what they will kill and how to apply them. Similarly, other smaller pests such as greenfly and blackfly should be vigorously controlled as they not only cause damage to young shoots but are also the means by which viruses are distributed.

Some pests, such as the vine weevil and narcissus fly larvae, attack the underground parts and these are less easy to control with chemicals. On a small scale the gardener can dig up his bulbs if they look at all unhealthy and burn any which are infested with grubs. With bulbs in pots it is easy enough to sort out the healthy bulbs at repotting time. Narcissus flies lay their eggs in early summer on the dormant bulbs; when the foliage dies away, make sure the ground is hoed over to close the holes left by the withered leaves, thus blocking access down to the bulbs.

Diseases are a worse problem in that they can get a hold before they are noticed. For the amateur grower botrytis (grey mould) is one of the worst problems, especially with bulbs growing in winter and early spring in frames and greenhouses where the air does not circulate too freely. Keeping the foliage as dry as possible helps, and there should be as much air movement as possible. Any infected leaves should be removed, and spraying with one of the several fungicides on the market will assist in the control. Lilies may get botrytis during wet weather in summer; it attacks the leaves, causing brown or transparent patches and death of the leaf, and sometimes also moves into the stem, causing it to keel over.

If cultural conditions are right, in particular good drainage, there should be few problems with the bulbs themselves, but there is one nasty disease of *Iris reticulata* and its relatives called ink disease; black resting bodies are visible when the bulbs or corms are handled at repotting or planting time. The infected bulbs should be removed and the rest should be soaked in a 'dip' of benomyl (e.g. Benlate) solution, diluted to the manufacturer's instructions.

Viruses, the effects of which can usually be seen in the distortion of the flowers, light and dark streaks in the leaves or stunting and distortion of the whole plant, are, for the gardener, incurable. The only way to discourage their spread is to burn infected plants, to control aphids, which act as the agents of dispersal for viruses, and to avoid handling 'clean' plants immediately after touching infected ones. Some nurseries offer virus-free stocks of, for example, lilies, but it is an expensive and complicated business to rid a stock of virus and the bulbs will probably cost substantially more than 'ordinary' stocks. For the amateur, raising new stock from seed is a way out of this problem, as seedlings fortunately do not normally inherit viruses from the parent.

On the whole, if cultural conditions are excellent then the plants will stand a much better chance of staying healthy. Poor, weak specimens are far more likely to succumb, so, first and foremost, try to get the cultivation technique right.

Iris reticulata varieties are normally easy to grow, but the bulbs can be destroyed by ink disease

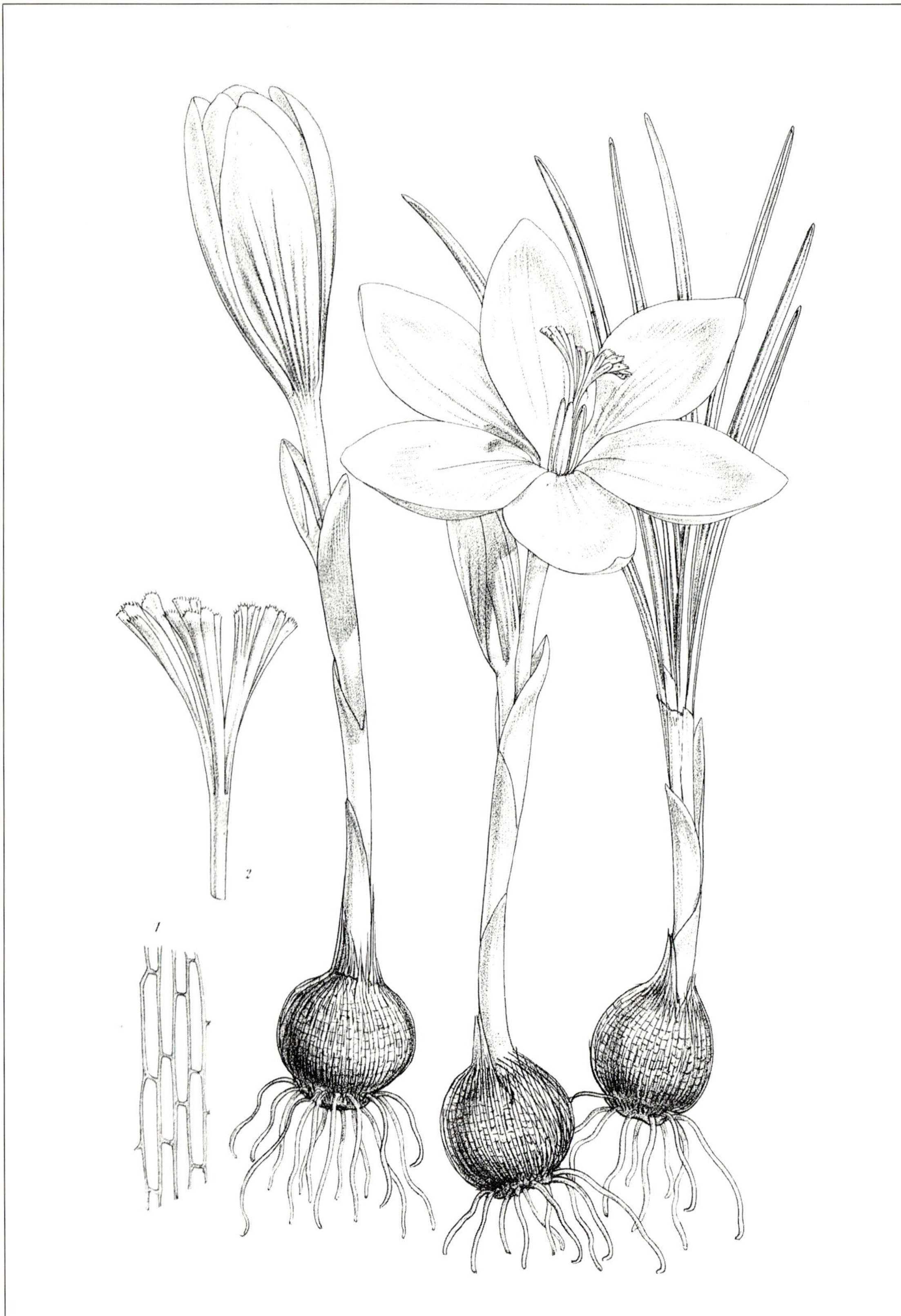
2
1

5
Special Bulbs for the Enthusiast

Sooner or later anyone who becomes deeply interested in the plants they grow will want to try some of the more unusual bulbs. In general these are less frequently seen in nurseries and gardens, either because they are not so easy to grow in open ground or because they are less easily propagated. As a general rule anything with a hint of rarity is more expensive to buy, and for most people this means that only a few bulbs of each, perhaps only one, will be purchased. It is therefore particularly important that the cultivation methods offer a good chance of success.

Bulbs that do not thrive in the open garden are usually those that require a definite warm, dry rest period, which the cooler northern countries cannot guarantee, or they may be plants that produce fragile or very small flowers during the most inclement months and thus require protection if they are going to be seen to the best advantage. The cold frame and unheated greenhouse both provide suitable conditions for growing such bulbs, and can make a delightful feature in the enthusiast's garden, providing interest at a time of year when there is little to be seen elsewhere. In the case of the greenhouse they can be viewed in relative comfort whatever the weather. Expense will usually be the main factor in deciding whether to have a frame or greenhouse for this purpose, as from the point of view of access to the plants and general comfort the latter wins every time. In the greenhouse one can walk about freely in the dry to inspect, weed, repot or photograph one's bulbs at leisure, whereas unless the frame is built very high off the ground there is a lot of bending and crawling about to be done, sometimes in the pouring rain or freezing cold. However, the frame does provide a much cheaper method of growing a large number of unusual bulbs and one may not want a greenhouse dominating the garden.

In the cold frame bulbs can be grown either in pots or planted directly into the soil, whereas in a greenhouse they are nearly always kept in pots, though there is actually no reason why bulb beds should not be constructed within the house. With pots there is the advantage of having individual control over the growing conditions of the bulbs, but on the other hand it takes a lot of work to maintain a collection in vigorous health, and many species soon deteriorate if they are not looked after properly. Another advantage of pot cultivation is that there is less chance of getting bulbs mixed up than there is when they are planted in a bed. It is also easy to move pots around for a better display or for closer inspection, and they can be made readily accessible for photography. Planted in bulb frames or greenhouse beds they are a little less accessible and there is slightly less control over their separate requirements. There is, too, always the chance that different varieties may increase and grow into each other, becoming mixed. On the whole it is a matter of personal preference as to which method is adopted: if the prime consideration is the health and vigour of the bulbs then planted bulb frames or beds have the advantage; if accessibility is considered important, cultivation in pots provides the most useful method.

Opposite:
Crocus cancellatus, a botanical drawing by W.H. Fitch. The style (2) is shown in detail

FLOWERING BULBS FOR THE GARDEN

Opposite:
Zephyranthes candida, a lovely autumn bulb for a sunny wall or, in cold districts, a greenhouse or bulb frame

Below:
Calochortus albus is one of a fascinating group of American bulbs for the specialist to try in a bulb frame or alpine house

CULTIVATION IN POTS

Unless very large quantities are required it is easiest to obtain potting composts ready mixed from a local supplier. For a collection of unusual bulbs loam-based composts such as John Innes No. 1 give better results, in my experience, than loamless ones. To three parts of the compost add one part of coarse gritty sand to ensure extra sharp drainage. Clay pots (not shallow pans) with some broken crocks in the bottom are my personal choice, but plastic ones can be used with success, though the soil in plastic ones can stay wet and cold during dull, damp weather whereas clay pots tend to dry out much more rapidly. Another enemy of bulbs in pots is frost, as they are generally grown without any heat in frames or greenhouses, and it is essential to plunge the pots up to their rims in some sharply drained material, of which coarse sand is usually the most easily obtainable. Pots which are not plunged can become frozen solid right to the bottom in severe weather, and many otherwise hardy bulbs can be killed by this. In frames such a plunge bed is simple to make. It is less easy to arrange on a greenhouse bench, and it may be preferable to remove the staging and make a low brick bed at ground level. Initial potting or repotting should take place in late summer or early

Special Bulbs for the Enthusiast

autumn for the winter-growing Mediterranean-type bulbs (see page 21) which flower between autumn and spring, and in spring for the summer-flowering bulbs. There are very few hardy summer growers suitable for growing in pots, and if any are grown they should be kept separate from the others as their dormant period falls in a different season and they therefore have different watering needs.

The bulbs are best placed about half way down the pot, as most bulbs deteriorate rapidly if planted near the surface. During active growth, especially with strong-growing types, feeding is beneficial and this can be given as a liquid fertilizer once a fortnight or as a slow-release pelleted fertilizer scattered on the surface, following the instructions on the pack. Those with a very high nitrogen content must be avoided; the one I use has nitrogen/phosphate/potassium (NPK) proportions of 15:15:30. Watering depends upon the weather and the needs of individual plants, but in general the pots should be kept just damp from potting time until early spring, when growth begins more strongly, and then plenty of water should be given until the leaves begin to die back in early summer, when it should be progressively reduced to nil during the dormant period. In very hot weather it may be necessary to shade the frames to prevent the resting bulbs from becoming too hot and dessicated; bulbs which prefer cool shade, such as snowdrops and dog's-tooth violets, must not be dried out completely and 'cooked' in the sun. A great many bulbs, however, require a warm, dry rest period in order to ripen and form flower buds for the following season, and in this category fall the bulbous irises, most dwarf narcissus, many crocus species and the tulip species. Ventilation must be good at all times, especially when the bulbs are in active growth, but it is best to close down the frames during very frosty weather in the winter.

Cultivation in bulb frames and greenhouse beds

Much the same comments apply to planted-out bulbs as to cultivation in pots. The main difference, provided that the beds were well made in the first place and that growth is satisfactory, is that the bulbs can be left in the same position for several years; it is thus worth the effort of thorough preparation. The frames or beds can be simple structures of brick, concrete or even wood, as long as it is thick and well treated with a preservative; railway sleepers are suitable, but are becoming less easy to obtain. The height is not too important, but somewhere between 20 and 45 cm (8–18 in) above the surrounding soil level is a guide; raised to this extent, the bed will provide good sharp drainage if filled with the correct materials. On sandy soils no extra drainage will be necessary at the bottom of the bed but on clay a layer of clinker, broken brick rubble or coarse gravel is advisable, at least 5 cm (2 in) deep. The soil filling, if it is a small frame, can be ready mixed John Innes No. 1 compost, but this is expensive for a large bed and one can either buy separate loam and add moss peat and coarse sand in the proportions two loam, one peat, one sand or, instead of loam, use the existing garden soil and add peat and sand in the same quantities. The main disadvantage, unless sterilized loam can be obtained or you have the equipment to sterilize it yourself, is that weeds will spring up in great quantity in the ideal conditions provided by the frame. Frequent, diligent weeding in the first few months can, however, soon reduce these, and if the weather is good the sun baking in summer will further reduce the problem.

Winter-growing/summer-dormant bulbs are planted in early autumn. As mentioned under pot cultivation, the planting depth is important; most bulbs need to be at least 5 cm (2 in) below the surface, though there are a few exceptions to this rule, such as the tuberous anemones and cyclamen. After the bed is planted up it should be given a good watering to settle the sil around the bulbs and then be kept just moist, with a lot of air through the frame or greenhouse, through the autumn. In winter there will be little need for watering and this should be as infrequent as possible, just enough to stop the bulbs drying out completely. As soon as any mild weather arrives and aerial growth becomes active more water can be given. Although frame lights can be removed on fine days, or the greenhouse opened up completely, on frosty nights protection must still be given until the danger of sharp frosts has passed; after this full ventilation all the time is best and frame lights can be removed completely, except during heavy storms. In late spring, when there are signs that the growth cycle is nearing an end and the foliage is beginning to wither, the frames can be replaced and water reduced.

Summer-growing/winter-dormant bulbs need the reverse watering and drying treatment, of course, and they are normally planted in spring. The frame lights should be kept on in winter for rain and frost protection, and no water is given. In late spring the bulbs are started into growth by slight watering, and full ventilation is provided in the frame (or greenhouse) through the summer growth period, with plenty of water available during hot spells. When the foliage begins to die back in autumn, water is progressively withheld until they are completely dormant.

These two different types of bulbs (i.e. winter and summer growers) should not be mixed, and it is best to have a separate bed for each. When planting such collections of bulbs it is also preferable not to place two very similar ones together so as to avoid the danger of mixing them up when lifting and replanting. For example, the bulbs of narcissus species all look much alike and might be confused if they spread into each other, but if they are separated by a patch of crocus corms or fritillaria bulbs the chances of a mix-up are very slight. It is also wise to collect all the seed from the bulbs before it falls naturally and to sow it separately (see page 49); a bulb bed left to its own devices soon becomes a chaotic mixture, usually with the most common, least interesting bulbs taking over and crowding out the more unusual ones.

If names are of interest then labels must be provided, or a careful planting plan made. With a collection of rare bulbs it is best to do both in case birds or the neighbour's cat remove or dig up the labels. Sooner or later one is likely to become involved in exchanging rare bulbs with friends, as it is the only way of acquiring quite a lot of them, and then it is important that their names and origins have been kept. Carefully labelled bulbs are also much easier to find when they are dormant!

Lists of bulbs suitable for growing in unheated frames and greenhouses appear on page 118.

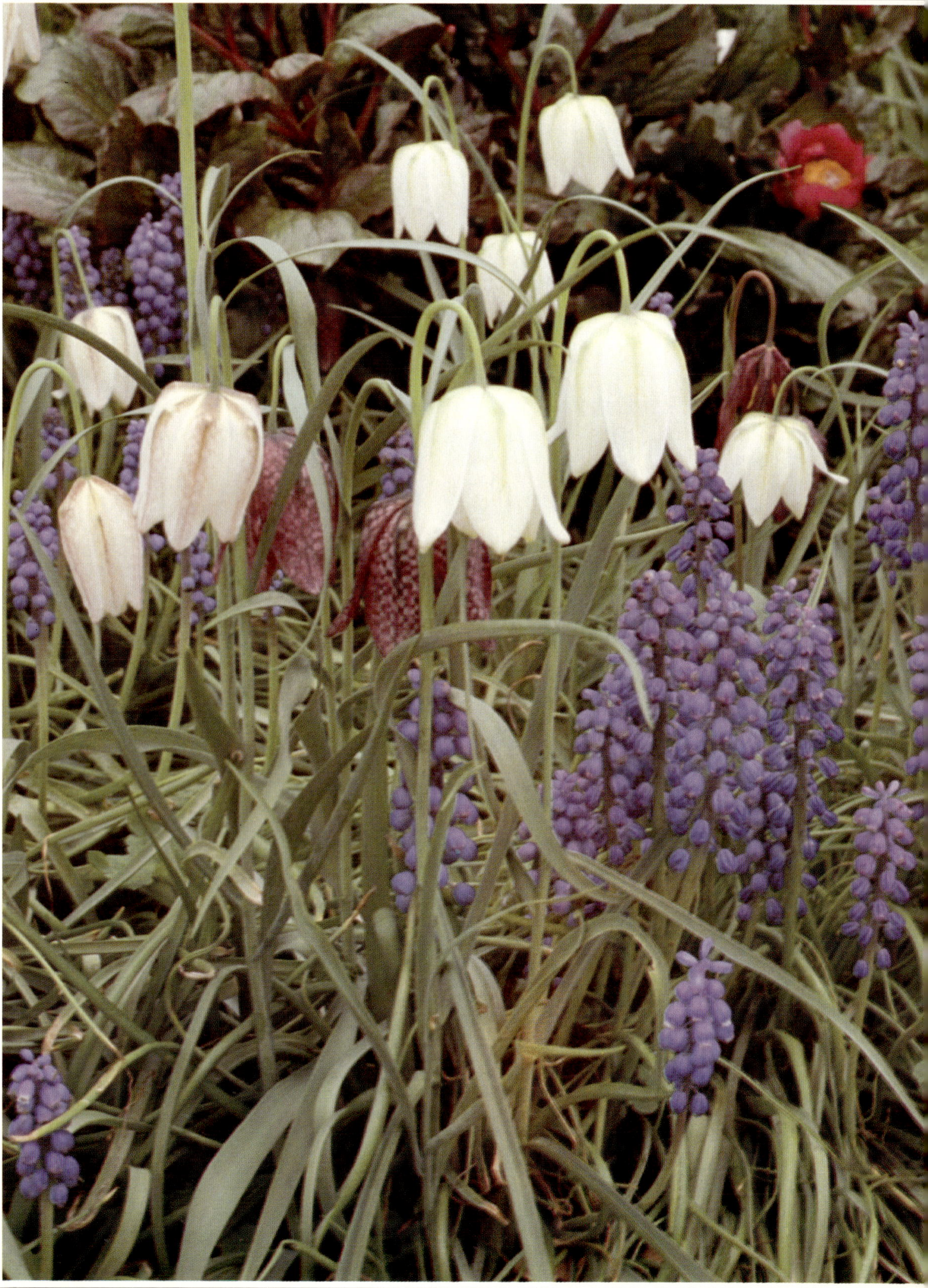

A to Z of Flowering Bulbs

A charming informal mixture of snakeshead
fritillaries and grape hyacinths

Allium

A very large group distributed throughout the northern hemisphere and mainly known for its culinary members such as onion, leek and garlic. Alliums are characterized by having smallish flowers in an umbel, and most have a distinct onion smell when crushed. Many species are non-bulbous and the majority have little ornamental value, but there are several attractive bulbous species worth cultivating, ranging from dwarf ones for the rock garden to tall border plants. The following species, which offer a selection right across the range, should be planted in autumn in open, sunny, well-drained situations unless otherwise stated.

A. aflatunense One of the easiest of the tall Asiatic 'drumstick' alliums, growing 60–90 cm (2–3 ft) in height with many starry, lilac-purple flowers in dense umbels 10–12 cm (4–5 in) in diameter in May or June.

A. caeruleum Blue is unusual for an allium, so this is an interesting variation. The 30–60 cm (1–2 ft) stems bear tight umbels, 3–4 cm (about 1½ in) in diameter, of small, bright blue flowers in mid summer. Central Asia.

A. callimischon Few alliums bloom in autumn, so this dwarf Cretan species is useful for the rock garden. It makes clumps of bulbs and tufts of 10 cm (4 in) stems carrying small umbels of papery, whitish flowers spotted with red.

A. carinatum subsp. ***pulchellum*** (*A. pulchellum*) A late summer European species, most elegant with slender 30–40 cm (12–16 in) stems and medium-sized umbels of pendent purple or white ('Alba') flowers which become erect in fruit.

A. christophii (*A. albopilosum*) This Asiatic species has large, shiny, metallic-looking lilac-purple flowers in enormous umbels about 10–20 cm (4–8 in) in diameter on stout stems 25–50 cm (10–20 in) in height. After flowering in summer the heads become stiff and spiky and are ideal for winter decorations.

A. flavum This is like a yellow version of *A. carinatum* subsp. *pulchellum* (above). It is a summer-flowering southern European species, and though it is usually 20–25 cm (8–10 in) in height there are also dwarf forms in cultivation as 'Minus' or 'Nanum'.

A. giganteum One of the largest species 1–1.5 m (3 ft–5 ft) in height, in summer bearing masses of violet flowers in dense umbels 10–15 cm (4–6 in) in diameter. Although from Central Asia it is slightly tender and requires a sheltered spot in sandy soil.

A. karataviense Although only 15–20 cm (6–8 in) tall, this Asiatic species has large umbels of pale pink flowers, up to 15–20 cm (6–8 in) in diameter in May or June. The beautiful broad, greyish-purple leaves make it a most striking plant for the front of a border.

A. moly Of the yellow-flowered alliums this European woodland species is both the easiest and the best for garden value; it is 15–25 cm (6–10 in) tall with a 5–7 cm (2–3 in) diameter umbel of large golden flowers carried above greyish leaves in summer. It is useful for naturalizing among shrubs.

A. neapolitanum A slightly tender Mediterranean species best given full sun near a south-facing wall. It grows 20–30 cm (8–12 in) in height with loose, 5–7 cm (2–3 in) diameter umbels of large white flowers in May or June.

A. oreophilum (*A. ostrowskianum*) This dwarf Asiatic species is probably the most attractive for the rock garden as it is only 10–15 cm (4–6 in) tall, with 4–6 cm (about 2 in) diameter umbels of deep rose flowers in May or June. The selection 'Zwanenburg' has deeper carmine flowers.

A. rosenbachianum Another of the Asiatic 'drumstick' alliums, with many small purple flowers in spherical umbels up to 10 cm (4 in) diameter on 50–100 cm (20–40 in) stems in May or June. The similar *A. stipitatum* is sometimes confused with this.

ANEMONE

weed. It has broad, elliptical leaves and 15–25 cm (6–10 in) stems with 4–5 cm (up to 2 in) diameter umbels of small white flowers in early summer.

Allium moly

AMARYLLIS

A large autumnal bulb, flowering before the leaves appear. Although South African it is hardy in sunny borders by a south wall, and needs a good warm, dry spell in summer to induce it to flower well. Plant the bulbs about 5–10 cm (2–4 in) deep.

A. belladonna This is the only species, reaching about 50–90 cm (20–36 in) in height with an umbel of large, pink, funnel-like scented flowers. The leaves stay green through the winter and may need some protection in severe winters.

ANEMONE

The anemones are mainly herbaceous perennials, but a few of the smaller tuberous and rhizomatous species are stocked by bulb nurseries. They include the important florists' varieties, 'De Caen' and 'St Brigid', and several very good rock garden plants such as A. blanda and the A. nemorosa varieties, which are also good for naturalizing.

A. apennina An easily grown European mountain plant, 10–15 cm (4–6 in) tall with ferny leaves and many-petalled blue flowers in spring. In semi-shade and humus-rich soil its rhizomes form patches which can be divided just after flowering. 'Alba' has white flowers.

A. blanda This popular Greek spring anemone is 5–10 cm (2–4 in) tall with graceful dissected leaves and variously coloured flowers with ten to twenty petals. In addition to the ordinary blue form there is 'Atrocaerulea' (dark blue), 'Charmer' and 'Pink Star' (pink), 'Radar' (magenta) and 'White Splendour'. The tubers are planted in autumn 3–4 cm (a good 1½ in) deep in sun or partial shade, where they can be left undisturbed to naturalize.

A. roseum In its best forms this is most attractive, with large, bright pink flowers in umbels 5–7 cm (2–3 in) diameter that are produced in early summer on 25–40 cm (10–16 in) stems. Being a Mediterranean species, it requires a sheltered, sunny position.

A. sphaerocephalon Although not of impressive size this is an interesting European species, with its very tight, dark purple umbels 2–3 cm (1–1½ in) in diameter looking like small drumsticks on 40–70 cm (16–28 in) stems.

A. triquetrum This European species can be invasive, but it is attractive for naturalizing in cool, shady places under trees or shrubs. The 15–20 cm (6–8 in) stems carry few-flowered umbels of bell-shaped white flowers in April or May.

A. ursinum A British native ('Ramsons') which should only be introduced to the garden if there is plenty of room for naturalizing in damp shade as it can be a

Anemone nemorosa 'Allenii'

A. coronaria The Mediterranean poppy anemone has given rise to the lovely 'St Brigid' and 'De Caen' varieties in shades of blue, white, red and violet, single or semi-double, with a central dark mass of stamens. The leaves are rather parsley-like. An autumn planting gives flowers in spring, or the tubers can be planted in spring for flowering in summer. A sheltered, sunny site in rich soil is necessary with the tubers about 3–4 cm (a good 1½ in) deep.

A. fulgens This is very like *A. coronaria* but has less divided leaves. The bright scarlet spring flowers have a few broad petals, or many narrow ones in the variety 'Multipetala'. It needs the same treatment as the poppy anemone.

A. nemorosa The spring-flowering ferny-leaved native wood anemone likes cool shade with a leafmould-rich soil, and is good for naturalizing beneath shrubs, its stick-like rhizomes soon forming patches. The common form is white but several lovely forms have been selected including the blue 'Robinsoniana', 'Allenii' and 'Blue Bonnet', and a double white. The rhizomes must not be dried out; they are best divided after flowering and should be planted only just beneath the surface.

A. pavonina In its appearance and cultivation needs the peacock anemone from Greece is very similar to *A. coronaria* (above), but the leaves are less finely dissected. The colour range is very wide, especially in the famous 'St Bavo' anemones, which are good for cutting.

A. ranunculoides This is like a yellow version of the wood anemone and requires similar conditions. It is a delightful plant for semi-shade on a rock garden or under shrubs, both in its single form and the double 'Flore Pleno'.

ANOMATHECA

A small genus of South African cormous plants, only one of which is at all hardy.

A. laxa This little summer-flowering species has a flat fan of leaves and 10–30 cm (4–12 in) stems bearing red flowers blotched darker red in the throat; there is also a white form 'Alba'. A sunny sheltered position is best.

ARISAEMA

A large, interesting genus related to the arums, only a few species of which are in general cultivation. The large tubers give rise to stout stems carrying attractively divided leaves and, in summer, the green to purple or (rarely) white hooded spathes. They are best planted in spring about 10 cm (4 in) deep.

A. candidissimum From China this is probably the best, having beautiful white spathes in June or July striped with pink and green, about 15 cm (6 in) tall including the short stem, and overtopping the leaves. After flowering the three-lobed leaves expand considerably and require a lot of room. It is very hardy and does well in dampish situations or any sunny spot provided that there is plenty of moisture in summer.

A. consanguineum A very vigorous eastern Asiatic species reaching a metre in height when growing well, with spotted stems crowned by the leaves which are attractively divided into many narrow leaflets. The large spathes produced in June or July are green with purple lines, and are usually followed by clusters of red berries in autumn. It does best in semi-shade in humus-rich soil.

ARISARUM

One species in this small group of relatives of the cuckoo pint (arum) is worth growing just for fun, for it is not at all showy.

A. proboscideum From Spain and Italy. It produces a low ground cover of deep green arum-like leaves, and in spring small, plump, blackish spathes which have a long tail-like apex, hence the popular name of 'mouse plant'. It is easy to grow in semi-shade in a humus-rich soil.

Arum creticum

ARUM

For the bulb specialist these curious plants known as lords and ladies or cuckoo pint may have a fascination, but for the majority of gardeners they are not striking enough to be of aesthetic value. A few species are, however, excellent garden plants. The tubers should be planted 10 cm (4 in) deep.

A. creticum A Cretan species rather rare in cultivation but easy to grow in a sunny, sheltered position. The plain green leaves appear in autumn and are overtopped in spring by bright yellow spathes which, unlike many arums, have a sweet fragrance.

A. italicum In its form known as 'Pictum' this is a most useful European species, producing bold arrow-shaped leaves in autumn, which last right through the winter and spring; they are deep green with conspicuous creamy veins and are ideal for flower arrangements or for livening up semi-shaded borders in winter. In spring there are pale green spathes, followed by spikes of red berries.

BRIMEURA

A small genus formerly included in *Hyacinthus*, but looking more like squills (scilla). One of the two species is well worth growing in the rock garden or in semi-shade beneath shrubs.

B. amethystina (*Hyacinthus amethystinus*) A Pyrenean native about 15 cm (6 in) high, with narrow basal leaves and a raceme of brilliant blue, tubular flowers, each about 1 cm (½ in) long, produced in May or June; there is a white form, 'Alba'. The bulbs are obtained and planted in autumn 3–4 cm (a good 1½ in) deep.

Brodiaea (and Triteleia)

I have combined these two genera here as the species are to be found in catalogues and literature in either genus. They are best in sunny, sheltered positions as they are not very hardy; the corms are planted in autumn or spring about 5 cm (2 in) deep in well-drained soil. They are from the western United States, and all of them flower in early summer.

B. ixioides (*Triteleia ixioides*) Stems about 15–25 cm (6–10 in) tall carry 10 cm (4 in) diameter loose umbels of starry yellow flowers that have a purplish stripe along the centre of each perianth segment.

B. lactea (*T. hyacinthina*) Smaller, more dense umbels of white flowers on stems 25–30 cm (10–12 in) in height.

B. laxa (*T. laxa*) This is one of the best, having deep blue flowers up to 3 cm (1¼ in) across in large, loose, many-flowered umbels up to 15 cm (6 in) diameter. *B. × tubergenii*, a hybrid of *B. laxa*, is very similar, as is *B.* 'Queen Fabiola', which is currently offered in bulb catalogues.

Bulbocodium

This European mountain plant is related to *Colchicum* and has similarly upright, wine-glass shaped flowers at ground level, and a similar corm.

B. vernum Bright reddish-purple flowers 3–4 cm (a good 1½ in) in diameter, produced in spring just before the rosette of lanceolate leaves appears. It requires a sunny, well-drained spot and is suitable for a rock garden.

Calochortus

This is a large group of fascinating and beautiful bulbs in the lily family from the western United States and Mexico. They are unfortunately mostly rather difficult to grow and require careful treatment in a bulb frame or alpine house. For this reason they are seldom obtainable from nurseries and mainly have to be acquired privately through exchange. The American species are spring-flowering, the Mexican flower in late summer. A few examples of the commonest and easiest are:

C. albus Stems about 15–20 cm (6–8 in) tall, carrying several pendent, white, globe-shaped flowers, lined inside with hairs. Plant in autumn in the bulb frame or alpine house.

C. barbatus (*Cyclobothra lutea*) One of the Mexican species, dormant in winter and flowering in August or September, so the bulbs are planted in spring. Several pendent yellow bells, lined with hairs, are produced on branched 15–20 cm (6–8 in) stems. It is hardy in many southern areas and prefers a sunny border.

C. luteus A gorgeous species 20–30 cm (8–12 cm) tall with large, upward-facing flattish flowers 3–4 cm (a good 1½ in) across with the three large petals often blotched brown at the base. A spring-flowering species for the alpine house or bulb frame.

C. uniflorus This is one of the easiest to grow, increasing well in the alpine house or frame. It is 10–15 cm (4–6 in) high with several flowers in May, upward facing and in a delicate shade of soft lilac.

Camassia

Early summer-flowering bulbs from North America which resemble very large squills, with long racemes of starry blue flowers. They require sunny or semi-shaded places which are not too dry, and may also be grown in rough grass. The bulbs need to be planted about 7–10 cm (3–4 in) deep in autumn.

C. leichtlinii Produces tall racemes, to nearly a metre (over 3 ft), of many large, starry blue flowers over grey-green, linear leaves. 'Atrocaerulea' has deep violet-blue flowers.

C. quamash (*C. esculenta*) Shorter in stature at about 40–45 cm (16–18 in) with rich blue flowers in dense racemes.

CARDIOCRINUM

This amazing relative of the lilies is a Himalayan plant of enormous proportions, requiring a considerable amount of space if it is to be seen effectively. *C. giganteum* is the only species generally available and this should be planted when obtained, usually in autumn, with the tips of the bulbs level with the surface of the soil. A sheltered, semi-shaded position should be chosen in soil which is rich in humus to a depth of 60 cm (2 ft – about two spades) or more, and which remains cool and moist in summer.

C. giganteum Reaches 2–4 m (6 ft 6 in–13 ft) in height with huge, heart-shaped basal leaves and a stout leafy stem bearing at its tip several elegant, semi-pendent white trumpets 15–30 cm (6–12 in) long. After flowering in July and August the bulb dies, leaving several young offsets which can be planted out to grow on, flowering in about three or four years. The distance between the bulbs should be about a metre (3 ft 3 in) to allow the leaves to develop. Seeds are produced in quantity but these will take at least seven years to produce flowering bulbs.

CHIONODOXA

A small genus of mainly Turkish bulbs, related to scilla but easy to distinguish by the cone of stamens in the centre. They all have two basal leaves and short racemes to about 5–10 cm (2–4 in) of blue or purple flowers in early spring. The bulbs should be planted 3–4 cm (a good 1½ in) deep in sun or partial shade in well-drained soil. There is confusion over the names but these are currently accepted to be correct.

C. forbesii This is the most common chionodoxa, usually sold under the names *C. luciliae*, *C. siehei* or *C. tmoli*; these are various forms of the same species, which has bluish-lavender flowers with a white eye, carried in a one-sided raceme.

C. luciliae The true plant of this name is often sold under the synonym *C. gigantea*. It is distinctive in having only one or two large, upward-facing lilac flowers.

C. sardensis This has several flowers in a raceme, like *C. forbesii*, but they are of a much clearer, deep blue.

COLCHICUM

These cormous plants, looking like large crocuses, are either autumn- or spring-flowering, though few of the latter are in general cultivation. The autumn-flowering ones are mostly leafless, producing large foliage in the spring so they need careful siting where they will not swamp other things. They will grow well in full sun or slight shade, and the more vigorous ones are attractive in grass. Plant in autumn with the corms about 10 cm (4 in) deep in reasonably well-drained soil.

Cardiocrinum giganteum

FLOWERING BULBS FOR THE GARDEN

Camassia quamash

Colchicum speciosum

C. × agrippinum An early autumn hybrid colchicum, usually August or September, with attractive smallish, rosy lilac flowers with a distinctly tessellated pattern. The leaves are fairly small so it is a good plant for a mixed sunny border.

C. autumnale The well-known British meadow saffron, which is good for naturalizing in grass or among shrubs. The small, pinkish-lilac long-tubed flowers are produced in early autumn long before the lush, glossy leaves. There is a double, 'Pleniflorum', a white, 'Album' and a double white, 'Alboplenum', all of which are worthwhile variants.

C. bivonae (*C. sibthorpii*, *C. bowlesianum*) This is probably the best of the leafless autumn species, with large, goblet-shaped pink flowers, strongly tessellated darker; unfortunately it is rather rare in cultivation. The flowers can be 15 cm (6 in) in height, much larger than those of *C. autumnale*. It occurs in Italy, Greece and Turkey.

C. byzantinum A plant of unknown origin but a very useful floriferous garden plant. Each corm produces several bright, rosy lilac flowers in early autumn, of good substance and withstanding inclement weather quite well. The robust leaves appear in spring.

C. cilicicum From southern Turkey, but very hardy and excellent for any sunny border where there is room for the large foliage to develop. Up to twenty flowers may be produced in early autumn, deep rosy lilac goblets with strong perianth tubes and broad overlapping segments.

C. luteum One of the few spring-flowering species to be offered in the specialist bulb lists, and extraordinary because of its yellow flowers produced in early spring together with the leaves. It is a high mountain plant from the western Himalaya requiring a well-drained position in a raised bed or rock garden or, better still, alpine house cultivation.

C. speciosum A superb autumn species from Turkey and the Caucasus, with very large, strong flowers in pale to deep pinkish-purple. There is a lovely white form, 'Album', which is one of the best of all autumn bulbs. It is a striking species for planting in quantity in sunny or semi-shaded places where the corms can be left undisturbed to increase at will and where there is room for the foliage.

Hybrids In addition to the wild species there are many excellent hybrids, but only a few of these are generally available from nurserymen. A selection that can usually be found are:
'Conquest' – purple flowers, strongly tessellated;
'Princess Astrid' – purple with a white centre;

66

'Lilac Wonder' – large rosy-purple flowers;
'Violet Queen' – dark purple throughout;
'The Giant' – rosy-lilac flowers with a white centre;
'Waterlily' – double lilac-mauve flowers.

CORYDALIS

This very large group of plants is related to the poppies, though it differs markedly from them in having irregular two-lipped flowers with a distinct spur, giving them a miniature snapdragon appearance. Many are annuals or herbaceous perennials, but there are also some tuberous-rooted spring-flowering species which are most attractive for the rock garden or for naturalizing. They are planted in autumn about 4–5 cm (1½–2 in) deep.

C. bulbosa (*C. cava*) A vigorous, easy European species for naturalizing beneath shrubs in humus-rich soil. The dissected, greyish leaves are overtopped by 15–20 cm (6–8 in) dense racemes of purplish, long-spurred flowers in March or April.

C. cashmeriana This Himalayan species is one of the most striking of all, needing cool, humid growing conditions in spring and summer. It forms 10–20 cm (4–8 in) clumps of finely divided leaves and has short spikes of brilliant blue flowers in summer. It is much easier in western and northern areas, especially Scotland. The scaly 'bulbs' must never be dried out when transplanting.

C. diphylla This is a delicate-looking Himalayan plant with diffuse, greyish leaves with narrow leaflets and loose racemes of white, purple-tipped flowers on 10–15 cm (4–6 in) stems in spring. It is hardy, but is best in the alpine house.

C. solida This European is one of the best-known species, very free-flowering and easy to grow in the rock garden, for naturalizing beneath shrubs or as an alpine house plant. Its tubers make compact clumps of handsome greyish, dissected foliage and dense racemes of purplish, long-spurred flowers in early spring. There are now some superb variants of this with pink or red flowers, rather uncommon but becoming available. 'George Baker' has terracotta-coloured flowers and is one of the best of these, sometimes offered as *C. transsilvanica*.

Corydalis solida

CRINUM

These are summer-flowering bulbs of the amaryllis family, the only hardy ones being South African. The easiest and most readily obtainable is the hybrid *C.* × *powellii*, a good plant for the herbaceous border provided that it receives

Crinum powellii

plenty of sun and moisture in summer. The enormous bulbs, shaped like Indian clubs, are usually obtainable in spring and should be planted in good, well-drained garden soil, with humus added if it is inclined to be poor and somewhat dry in summer. The top of the neck of the bulb should be at ground level.

C. × powellii This produces a tuft of strap-like, bright green basal leaves, followed in late summer or early autumn by stout stems up to a metre in height bearing umbels of up to ten large pink flowers (white in var. *album*). These are funnel-shaped with a long slender tube and with the tips of the perianth segments curling backwards when fully open. The bulbs are best left undisturbed for as long as they are doing well.

CROCOSMIA

These are South African plants, though the hybrid *C. × crocosmiiflora*, the montbretia, is naturalized in many countries. They are summer-flowering members of the iris family, growing from gladiolus-like corms which increase rapidly to form compact clumps. These are usually obtained and planted in spring about 5–10 cm (4–6 in) deep in a sunny, well-drained position. Crocosmias are ideal subjects for the mixed or herbaceous border and are now available in a wide range of colourful hybrids. They all have fans of sword-like leaves, overtopped by branching spikes of flowers.

C. × crocosmiiflora The old-fashioned montbretia with its panicles of orange funnel-shaped flowers on 40–60 cm (16–24 in) stems is the best known, almost indestructible and often to be seen naturalized away from gardens. It is nevertheless a valuable plant for a late summer display and does well in dry, sunny places.

C. masonorum A stately herbaceous perennial reaching nearly a metre when in flower, with bold, pleated leaves and many large, wide open, reddish-orange flowers facing upwards from the horizontal branches of the panicles.

Hybrids There are some excellent modern hybrids, notably those from Bressingham Gardens, which combine bright flower colours with hardiness. Some are crosses with *Curtonus paniculatus*.
'Lucifer' – a *C. paniculatus* cross up to a metre (39 in) tall, with bright, flame-red flowers in June or July.
'Emily McKenzie' – a smaller plant to about 50–60 cm (20–24 in), with orange flowers marked with brown-red blotches in the centre.
'Jackanapes' – about 50–60 cm (20–24 in) has bicoloured sprays of flowers in yellow and orange.
'Solfatare' – an interesting variation, with bronze foliage and orange-yellow flowers.

CROCUS

The much-loved crocuses of spring need little introduction, but few people realize that nearly all the well-known large Dutch varieties, purple, white or striped, are variations of just one species, and that there are 89 other species (and many forms of these) in a wide range of colours and flowering time, from August through autumn and winter to April. Of course, quite a number of these are not in general cultivation, or are very rare or tricky to

Crocus goulimyi

grow, but at least a third are excellent garden plants capable of being successfully cultivated without the help of a frame or alpine house. Regardless of flowering time, the corms are obtained and planted in early autumn, and for most species a sunny position in well-drained soil is suitable; they make good subjects for a rock garden. However, a few will grow in semi-shaded, moister sites and some are good for naturalizing in grass; in the descriptions below, comments will be made about any such uses. The corms should be planted about 3–4 cm (a good 1½ in) deep.

I have divided them into two groups, autumn and spring, but in the case of *C. laevigatus* the flowering may continue from late autumn through winter and into February.

AUTUMN-FLOWERING SPECIES
Mostly September–November
Some autumn crocuses flower before their leaves appear.

C. banaticus (*C. iridiflorus*) A unique Romanian species, in that its lilac-blue flowers have three large outer perianth segments and three small, erect inner ones, so when fully open it looks rather like an iris flower. The leaves are produced after the flowers have finished. This one likes moist sites and is ideal for a peat garden or for semi-shaded sites between shrubs.

C. cancellatus An early autumn one from Greece and Turkey, flowering before its leaves emerge. The flowers, in the commercially available form (*C. c.* 'cilicicus') are slender and pale blue with darker veins. The corms are covered with coarsely netted coats.

C. goulimyi This Greek species is a most attractive one for a hot, sunny position, producing long-tubed, lilac-blue flowers together with the leaves. Usually the inner three segments are slightly paler than the outer.

C. hadriaticus A lovely white crocus from Greece, with a deep yellow throat and three scarlet stigmas; the greyish leaves appear with the flowers. A good form is sometimes offered as *C. h.* 'chrysobelonicus'.

C. kotschyanus (*C. zonatus*) This Turkish species is one of the earliest in autumn, usually flowering in September. It has leafless, pale lilac flowers with yellow blotches at the base of each perianth segment, giving a yellow eye in the centre. Var. *leucopharynx* has a white eye with no yellow in the throat; it is sometimes erroneously listed as *C. karduchorum*. There is also a lovely white form, *C. kotschyanus* 'Albus'.

C. laevigatus A very late Greek crocus which can be relied upon to flower during the depth of winter but usually starts in late autumn. The leaves appear first, followed by pale violet flowers strongly striped darker purple on the outside and with a yellow centre; they are also fragrant. This is the most frequently available form, known as 'Fontenayi', but the species varies from white to deep violet with or without stripes. A sheltered, sunny spot is best.

C. medius A colourful late autumn species from Italy, with purple flowers produced before the leaves. At the centre of the flower is a splash of bright orange from the mass of fine stigma branches.

C. niveus From southern Greece, an uncommon species for a sheltered, sunny place. It has large white or palest lilac flowers with a deep yellow throat and orange stigmas; the leaves come with the flowers.

C. nudiflorus As its name says, this Pyrenean crocus has no leaves at flowering time. The late autumn blooms have long, slender tubes and are a rich, deep purple with orange stigmas. It requires a moist soil and is good in grass; it is stoloniferous, and can therefore form patches when well suited.

C. ochroleucus A small-flowered Lebanese species flowering in late autumn just before or with the leaves. The flowers are white with a deep yellow centre; it increases rapidly by producing offsets.

Flowering Bulbs for the Garden

Crocus sieberi 'Firefly'

C. pulchellus One of the best and easiest of the autumn species, from the Balkans and Turkey. It has leafless blue flowers with a deep yellow throat, finely veined darker on the outside; the stamens are white and the finely dissected stigmas yellow or orange. There is a lovely white form, also with a yellow throat, called 'Albus'. It will grow in sun or semi-shade and is good for naturalizing.

C. sativus The saffron crocus, the spice being obtained from the three long, red stigma branches. The large flowers, produced with the leaves, come in mid-autumn and are purple, strongly veined darker and with a dark purple eye in the centre. It requires rich soil in full sun with the corms planted at least 10 cm (4 in) deep. It is known only as a cultivated plant.

C. serotinus Usually available as a subsp. *salzmannii* (*C. salzmannii*). This Spanish species produces large, pale lilac flowers with a yellow throat, together with the leaves. An easy, free-flowering crocus, increasing well into clumps.

C. speciosus Perhaps the best of the autumn crocuses, with long, elegant flowers produced before the leaves in late September to mid October. The stigma is a mass of slender orange branches. The commonest form is violet-blue, intricately veined darker. 'Conqueror' has deep blue flowers, 'Globosus' has rounded perianth segments in bright blue, 'Oxonian' is a very deep violet-blue, and 'Albus' is the very beautiful pure white form. *C. speciosus* increases well and is good for naturalizing.

C. tournefortii An unusual species from the Greek Islands, having soft blue flowers with a yellow throat, produced together with the flowers in late autumn. The stamens are white and the stigmas bright orange. It has the distinction that the flowers remain wide open on dull days. It needs a sheltered, sunny spot.

CROCUS

Crocus imperati

SPRING-FLOWERING SPECIES
Mostly January–April
All the spring crocuses produce their leaves at flowering time.

C. ancyrensis From Turkey near Ankara (Ancyra), a bright little species with several smallish orange flowers from each corm, often sold as 'Golden Bunch'. The corms have a net-like coat.

C. angustifolius (*C. susianus*) In the best and most commonly seen form this Crimean species has bright yellow flowers stained or striped with mahogany brown on the outside. It is sometimes called the 'Cloth of Gold' crocus.

C. biflorus An extremely widespread Mediterranean, Turkish and Russian species which is tremendously variable; some of its forms are offered in catalogues as *C. chrysanthus* varieties (see below). Typical *C. biflorus* has white flowers with a yellow throat and purple stripes on the outside; a form of this is sometimes offered as 'Argenteus'. 'Parkinsonii' is similar with strong stripes.

Another very striking variant is subsp. *alexandri* which is white inside with a strong violet stain on the outside but with no yellow in the throat. Subsp. *weldenii* is wholly white-flowered, someties with a flush of blue near the base, while the selection of this known as 'Fairy' is shaded greyish-blue on the outside.

C. chrysanthus The ordinary wild form of this Balkan and Turkish species is a yellowish-orange, but in cultivation there are many selections and hybrids have been made with *C. biflorus*. Some of the blue and white forms sold under the general name of *C. chrysanthus* are forms of *C. biflorus*, but to avoid confusion I will keep them here under *C. chrysanthus*. The characteristic feature of both species and their varieties is a corm tunic which splits into distinct rings at the base. Some of the best are:
'Advance' – a curious shade of yellow with a mauve staining outside;
'Bluebird' – a soft pastel blue, whitish inside;
'Blue Pearl' – delicate blue shading to darker blue at the base;
'Cream Beauty' – one of the best, rich cream with orange stigmas;
'E. A. Bowles' – a deep yellow, large-flowered vigorous form;
'Ladykiller' – striking white form with a rich violet exterior;
'Snowbunting' – white flowers with a yellow throat and orange stigmas;
'Zwanenberg Bronze' – a yellow form, with a lovely bronze exterior.

These are good for displays in pots in the alpine house, on a windowsill or planted on a rock garden.

C. corsicus One of the latest species to flower, with lilac flowers, strongly striped

Curtonus paniculatus

darker outside, often on a biscuit-coloured ground colour; the stigma is a bright scarlet in the best commercial form. It is Corsican in origin.

C. dalmaticus An easily cultivated Yugoslavian crocus with lilac flowers, feathered with darker veins outside on a buff ground; the throat is yellow.

C. etruscus This Italian species is somewhat similar in colour to *C. dalmaticus*, though botanically it is quite distinct. It has much broader leaves. The variety 'Zwanenburg' with a greyish, conspicuously veined exterior is often available.

C. flavus A species cultivated since the 16th century, rich yellow throughout with stiff, erect leaves. The true species is rarely seen but the common large Dutch yellow crocus ('Golden Yellow') is a hybrid of it, extremely useful for its vigorous growth and free-flowering nature. It is good for naturalizing in grass.

C. fleischeri An attractive, small-flowered Turkish species with white flowers stained purple towards the base on the outside and made colourful on the inside by the yellow throat and many bright orange stigmas. It needs a hot, sunny place.

C. imperati A large-flowered species from Italy with bicoloured flowers, buff with purple lines on the outside and bright purple inside with a yellow throat. Subsp. *suaveolens* is very similar. One of the best forms, 'De Jager', has excellent colouring.

C. minimus A late-flowering, small, deep violet crocus, stained or striped darker on the outside. The leaves are narrow and held upright. It comes from Sardinia and Corsica.

C. olivieri Another bright orange-yellow species from the Balkans and Turkey. This one has very broad leaves and six divisions of the stigma. Subsp. *balansae* (*C. balansae*) is similar but with bronze stripes or staining on the outside.

C. sieberi This is one of the best lilac-flowered spring species, with a deep yellow throat, very free flowering and easily cultivated. 'Firefly' and 'Violet Queen' are both good colour selections. 'Hubert Edelsten' is an unusual garden form with bands of purple and white. *C. sieberi* is a Greek species.

C. tommasinianus One of the commonest species in gardens, originating from Yugoslavia. The slender flowers are usually lilac-blue with a white tube, but white ('Albus') and reddish-purple forms have been selected, for example 'Whitewell Purple'. 'Ruby Giant' has rich purple flowers and is probably a hybrid. This is an excellent species for naturalizing beneath shrubs or among hellebores and snowdrops, and is the first to flower in January or February.

C. vernus This species has given rise to the large-flowered Dutch crocus which are often used in bowls for an early display indoors. It is a widespread plant in Europe, mainly the Alps, and is very variable, purple, white and striped. The horticultural selections of it are much larger than the wild forms and are excellent for naturalizing in grass or planting in borders where they will not be disturbed. The following is a selection of those being offered:

'Little Dorrit' – pale silvery lilac-blue, stained purple on the tube;
'Jeanne d'Arc', 'Kathleen Parlow' – pure whites with orange stigmas;
'Pickwick', 'Striped Beauty' – strongly striped and feathered on white background;
'Paulus Potter' – deep rich purple with a lacquer-like gloss;
'Queen of the Blues' – a lovely soft blue shade;
'Remembrance' – a warm purple stained darker on the tube.

These are all very good in bowls or in the garden.

CURTONUS

A South African genus of one species looking like a giant montbretia, and a most attractive, unusual herbaceous border plant for a sunny position. The corms can be planted in spring or autumn, 10 cm (4 in) deep in quite rich, well-drained soil.

C. paniculatus reaches 1–1.5 metres (3 ft 3 in–5 ft) when in flower, with broad, sword-shaped, pleated leaves and branching stems bearing many tubular orange-red flowers which are curved and rather hooded at the apex. It flowers for a long period during late summer.

Cyclamen

There are few lovelier plants than the cyclamen species. Several of them are hardy, and the rest are suitable for growing in pots in an alpine house or frame. They are not only attractive for their perfect miniature cyclamen flowers but also for their foliage, which is often mottled and zoned with light and dark patterns. They like well-drained, humus-rich soil in semi-shade.

C. cilicium Autumn-flowering. A Turkish species with small, pale pink flowers with a darker carmine spot at the mouth of the corolla. The heart-shaped leaves vary widely in the amount of silvery patterning. *C. mirabile* is very similar.

C. coum (*C. vernum*, *C. orbiculatum*) Winter to early spring. One of the most useful species, as it will produce its small, rich carmine-coloured flowers in the depths of winter. There is a white form 'Album' which, like the coloured forms, has a dark purple stain around the mouth. Some forms have their rounded leaves plain dark green, others attractively silver-zoned. It comes mainly from Turkey and the Caucasus.

C. hederifolium (*C. neapolitanum*) Autumn-flowering. This is the best-known species, originating in the Mediterranean region. Its pinkish or white ('Album') flowers are carried in great profusion in early autumn before the leaves unfold, and are followed by a mat of ivy-shaped leaves with attractive patterns. It is good for naturalizing beneath deciduous shrubs and will seed itself around.

C. purpurascens (*C. europaeum*) Summer- or autumn-flowering. Although producing only a few pink flowers at a time, this species from the eastern Alps can be in bloom for a long period and is very strongly scented. The rounded leaves vary a lot in their markings.

C. repandum Spring-flowering. A free-flowering species from Italy and Yugoslavia. The scented flowers are a pale pinkish-carmine with a darker red-purple stain at the mouth. It has angular leaves quite well marked with light and dark patterns. Needs a sheltered place.

In addition to these there are several other species available from specialist nurseries, but in most districts they need the protection of a frame or alpine house.

Cypella

Only one species of this South American genus is in general cultivation, and that is rather infrequently seen. They are related to tigridias, with short-lived, iris-shaped flowers produced in long succession. The one species described below is hardy in southern districts, but in areas where the ground freezes to some depth may need to be lifted for the winter and stored away from frost. A sunny, sheltered spot is best.

Cyclamen hederifolium

C. herbertii Grows to about 30–40 cm (12–16 in) when in flower, with sword-shaped pleated leaves and mustard-yellow flowers with three large outer petals and three small convoluted inner ones, spotted with purple. It produces lots of seeds, which can be grown to flowering in two to three years.

Dierama pulcherrimum

Dierama

These graceful summer-flowering members of the Iridaceae have corms which increase to form dense clumps, giving rise to tufts of tough, narrow leaves which are almost evergreen. They come from the eastern Cape and tropical Africa, but only a few species are hardy. They require damp situations and are ideal for growing near a garden pool.

D. pulcherrimum The name angel's fishing rod conveys the graceful appearance of this plant. The slender flower stems can reach up to two metres (6 ft 6 in) in height and arch over at the tips, holding the several pinkish-purple bells in a pendent position. Various colour forms have been named, but unfortunately few of these are available.

Dracunculus

An extraordinary tuberous-rooted Mediterranean plant belonging to the arum family, suitable for growing in a sheltered sunny place in mild districts, but unfortunately having a disgusting smell when in flower.

D. vulgaris Grows to about a metre (3 ft 3 in) in height, with an attractive, conspicuously blotched and striped stem and strikingly lobed leaves. In June the enormous maroon-purple spathes are produced, 30–45 cm (12–18 in) long, with an erect, dark, shiny spadix emerging from the centre. It is nothing if not dramatic!

Eranthis

The delightful little winter aconite flowers as soon as the winter shows signs of letting up, usually in late January or February. It is good for naturalizing in humus-rich soil in semi-shade where it will not become too hot and dry in summer. It can be planted in autumn while dormant or in spring when the flowers have finished. The tubers should not be dried out too much when transplanting.

E. hyemalis A European woodlander, about 5–10 cm (2–4 in) high, with upright, yellow, cup-like flowers surrounded by a 'collar' of dissected leaves. *E. cilicica* from Turkey is similar, but usually with bronzy leaves, and there is a superb hybrid between the two, *E.* × *tubergenii* 'Guinea Gold', which has much larger flowers than either.

Erythronium

The lovely dog's-tooth violets have curious elongated, pointed bulbs which do look rather like canine teeth. The best-known, *E. dens-canis*, is a European and Asiatic plant, but the majority of species come from the western states of North America. They are all plants for growing in the semi-shade in cool, humus-rich soil in places where they can be left undisturbed for several years, such as a peat garden or shrub border. They are obtained and planted while dormant in autumn, but the bulbs must never be dried out too drastically.

Eranthis cilicica

E. dens-canis This has beautifully blotched and marbled elliptic leaves and 8–15 cm (3–6 in) stems bearing solitary pendulous flowers with sharply reflexing tips. There are several colour forms from white to deep pinkish-purple, with zones of white or yellow and brown or purple markings in the centre; some are named but mixed collections are usually offered. It is good for naturalizing under shrubs or in grass.

E. hendersonii An unusual species from California, which has a pair of mottled leaves and up to ten pendent lilac flowers with deep purple centres, on stems 10–15 cm (4–6 in) tall.

E. oregonum An American species with two attractively mottled leaves and one to five creamy white, yellow-centred flowers. For garden purposes the lovely, vigorous and easily obtained E. 'White Beauty', which is very similar, is better.

E. revolutum This is like a pink-flowered version of 'White Beauty', the lovely yellow-centred, rose-pink blooms carried over attractively mottled foliage.

E. tuolumnense A very distinct Californian species with plain, bright yellowish-green leaves and one to four pendent yellow flowers. It is very easy to grow and increases well. 'Pagoda' is a hybrid of this

Erythronium tuolumnense

with one of the white-flowered species, and has paler yellow flowers with slightly marble-patterned leaves.

Eucomis

The 'pineapple flowers' are natives of South Africa, late summer-flowering and dormant in winter. They have relatively large bulbs, rosettes of large fleshy basal leaves and dense spikes of starry flowers, crowned by a cluster of leaf-like bracts, hence the pineapple analogy. There are quite a number of species but only one or two are readily obtainable. These are surprisingly hardy and can be grown in a sunny border or in tubs on the patio; in the latter case, however, they must be placed in a frost-free shed or greenhouse for the winter. The bulbs are usually offered in spring.

E. bicolor The most commonly encountered species, with 30–40 cm (12–16 in) spikes of pale green flowers, each with a purple margin to the segments. The stems are purple-spotted.

E. comosa (*E. punctata*) One of the more colourful species, often with a slightly pink tinge to the flowers and a purple ovary, giving a dark eye to each flower.

E. undulata (*E. autumnalis*) This has greenish-white flowers and undulate-margined leaves which are quite attractive.

E. zambesiaca The dwarf of the genus, only 20 cm (8 in) in height, with short, dense spikes of white flowers.

In addition to these species some hybrids are beginning to appear in cultivation, often with more colourful flowers and sometimes with strongly purple-tinged leaves.

Freesia

These are, of course, well-known cut flowers in the florists' shops, and are tender plants which naturally grow and flower through the winter months. They are not hardy enough to be cultivated without the protection of a heated greenhouse. However, some bulb nurseries offer treated corms which have been kept in a dormant state ready for planting out into a warm sunny place in late spring. These will grow through the summer and flower in about August, but will be killed by frost the following winter unless they are lifted and stored in a warm, dry place. They are usually available as a mixed collection of colours, being of hybrid origin.

Fritillaria

A large genus of attractive bulbous plants in the lily family, the best-known of which are the snakeshead fritillary and the crown imperial. Many of the others have pendent, bell-shaped flowers in greenish or purplish-brown colours, often conspicuously tessellated, and although not showy are of great interest and are popular with bulb enthusiasts. Only a small proportion of the species can be grown really successfully in the open garden, the rest being best treated as alpine house or bulb frame plants. The following are usually readily obtainable, but the small specialist bulb nurseries may have quite a number of other species available from time to time.

They are obtained and planted in autumn, and all flower in April or May.

Fritillaria imperialis

F. acmopetala A Turkish species growing to about 30 cm (12 in) in height, with narrow, scattered grey leaves and attractively shaped large green and brown bells with the tips flaring outwards. A good species for the rock garden or sunny border.

F. camschatcensis Grows wild in eastern Asia and Alaska. It is 20–35 cm (8–14 in) tall with whorls of glossy green leaves and between one and four flowers which are like wide open bells in a blackish, purple-brown hue. It needs cool growing conditions in humus-rich soil in semi-shade, so is good for a peat garden.

F. crassifolia A variable Turkish and Iranian species, which is usually not more than 10 cm (4 in) tall with greyish green leaves and one or two bells of green or brown covered with a tessellated pattern and with a green stripe along the centre of each segment. It is best in a raised bed, bulb frame or alpine house.

F. graeca This Greek species is a stocky plant to 20 cm (8 in) tall, with grey leaves and tubby pendent bells in brown with a very bold green band along each outer segment. Subsp. *thessala* is a taller, more vigorous grower with a whorl of three leaves overtopping the lightly tessellated flowers. *F. graeca* itself is best grown in a bulb frame or alpine house, but subsp. *thessala* is a good rock garden or sunny border plant.

F. imperialis Perhaps the best-loved of all fritillaries, very different from most with its stout stems up to a metre (3 ft 3 in) in height, usually with whorled, glossy green leaves on the lower half of the stem and crowned by an umbel of several large, orange-red bells which are overtopped by a cluster of leafy bracts. Inside each flower is a large drop of liquid nectar. There are various cultivars available such as 'Lutea Maxima', a lovely clear yellow, 'Aurora', orange and 'Rubra Maxima', a vigorous variety with reddish-orange flowers. Crown imperials like a fairly rich soil in full sun, but will grow in semi-shade if it dries out well in summer. The bulbs should be not less than 15–20 cm (6–8 in) deep, and require feeding with bonemeal in autumn.

F. lusitanica (*F. hispanica*) An easy species to grow in the rock garden. From the Iberian peninsula it grows to about 20–30 cm (8–12 in) tall, with narrow leaves and one or two pendent bells, usually brownish with a tessellated pattern, though it does vary considerably.

F. meleagris The snakeshead fritillary is a British native from moist meadows and is therefore good for naturalizing in grass, on the rock garden or between deciduous shrubs. It grows up to 30 cm (12 in) tall, with narrow grey leaves and usually one large, nodding, squarish bell, in various shades of pale to deep pinkish-purple with a very conspicuous tessellated pattern, or white with a faint green pattern. There are named forms such as 'Aphrodite' (white), 'Charon' (dark purple) and 'Saturnus' (light purple-red), but it is usually offered as a mixed collection.

F. pallidiflora A delightful and unusual species from Central Asia which is very hardy and will grow in a sunny, well-drained spot. The stout 15–30 cm (6–8 in) stems carry broad, very grey leaves and between one and four large pendent bells in pale yellow, speckled reddish inside.

F. persica A widespread and variable species in the Middle East. It is unusual in having long racemes of many smallish, conical flowers, in the best forms deep blackish-purple. The stems, up to a metre (3 ft 3 in) tall, are densely clothed with narrow, grey-green leaves. It needs a sheltered sunny position, grown in the same way as the crown imperial.

F. pontica From northern Turkey and Greece, this is an easy species for a semi-shaded position in the shrub border or rock garden. It grows to about 20–30 cm (8–12 in) tall, with grey, lanceolate leaves, the upper ones in a whorl overtopping the large, pale green bells, which have a flush of brown but no tessellation.

F. pyrenaica A vigorous species from the

Fritillaria pallidiflora

Pyrenees, growing to 30 cm (12 in) with narrow, slightly greyish leaves. The large pendent bells, usually between one and three, are deep purple-brown on the outside and shiny greenish-yellow inside, the tips of the segments often curling outwards to reveal this colour. It does well in semi-shade in undisturbed borders or the rock garden.

F. raddeana From Central Asia; this is similar in general appearance to the crown imperial (see *F. imperialis* above), but is slightly smaller in habit and its smaller flowers are pale greenish-yellow. It is a lovely species for a sunny, well-drained border.

F. uva-vulpis ('*F. assyriaca*') A smallish, Middle Eastern species growing to 15–20 cm (6–8 in) tall, with bright green leaves and usually one narrow, bell-shaped flower in dark purple with yellow tips to the segments. It will grow in a sunny rock garden but is best in a bulb frame or alpine house. It is easy to propagate, increasing rapidly by offsets.

F. verticillata Is a 40–60 cm (16–24 in) slender species from China and Japan, with whorls of narrow leaves, the upper ones of which are tendril-like and will cling to other plants for support. It has several pendent flowers, white, veined and flecked with green. It is easy to grow but is often not very free-flowering. *F. thunbergii* is very similar.

GALANTHUS

Snowdrops need little introduction, for they are all similar in overall appearance, with their pendent white flowers having three large outer perianth segments and three small inner ones with green tips. There are, however, a lot of subtle differences between the species and their many hybrids and selections, and to the enthusiast this is a fascinating and beautiful group of plants.

Snowdrops are best transplanted in the spring just after they have flowered, but are sometimes sold as dried bulbs in the autumn: the important thing is not to let them dry out too much while they are dormant or they may take some time to recover.

The best situation is in semi-shade in moist soil with plenty of water-retaining humus added if it is inclined to be dry. They associate very well with hellebores, aconites and *Crocus tommasinianus* for a late winter–early spring display.

G. byzantinus A broad-leaved, vigorous snowdrop from Turkey, with the edges of the leaves folded downwards in a characteristic way. The quite large flowers have a green spot on the apex of each of the inner segments. *G. plicatus* from the Crimea is very similar but has two green spots, one at the base and one at the apex of the inner segments.

G. caucasicus A Caucasian species with broad, grey-green leaves, not folded down at the margins. The large flowers have green spots only at the apex of the three inner petals, otherwise it is very like the giant snowdrop, *G. elwesii*. There is a very early variety, 'Hiemale' or 'Early Form', which is often in flower in November or December.

G. elwesii The giant snowdrop, so called because it is usually much larger than the common *G. nivalis*. The bold leaves are grey-green, usually somewhat broader towards the apex, and the long flowers have green blotches at the base and apex of each of the inner perianth segments. It is a native of Turkey.

G. ikariae and **G. latifolius** are so similar as to be almost indistinguishable, and from a garden point of view there is little to choose between them. The leaves are bright, glossy green without any greyish overlay. These contrast beautifully with the pure white flowers, which have green blotches only at the apex of the inner petals. They are natives of the eastern Greek islands, Turkey and the Caucasus.

G. nivalis The common snowdrop of British and European woodlands. In its ordinary wild form it is one of the smallest snowdrops, with narrow, grey-green leaves. The familiar pendent flowers have green spots only at the apex of each inner segment. There is a common double form, 'Flore Pleno'. In addition there are many cultivars, some of which are probably hybrids with other species (see under cultivars below).

G. reginae-olgae In appearance this Greek species differs mainly from *G. nivalis* in having dark green leaves with a grey stripe along the centre, but it differs from all other snowdrops in being autumn-flowering. The large flowers are produced before the leaves appear, usually in October. It requires more sun than the others.

Cultivars There are a very large number in cultivation and the selection available changes from year to year depending upon nursery stocks. The following are very good ones, usually available:
'Atkinsii' – probably one of the very best, a robust grower with tall stems and long, graceful flowers;
'Magnet' – the large flowers are carried on long, slender pedicels well away from the stem;
'Sam Arnott' – a beautiful scented form with large, perfectly formed flowers;
'Scharlokii' – unusual in having a spathe split into two parts which stand up like ears above the flower;
'Viridapicis' – an interesting variation in which the outer three perianth segments as well as the inner have a conspicuous green patch at the apex.

Galtonia candicans

GALTONIA

A small genus of Cape bulbs which are winter-dormant and flower in mid-summer. They are hardy only in areas where the ground does not freeze beyond the surface crust, so in cold districts must be lifted and stored in winter. They are best in a sunny position which is well supplied with moisture. The bulbs are obtained and planted in spring when the ground has begun to warm up. Only one species is regularly available and this is the showiest, the others having greenish flowers.

G. candicans Grows to a metre or more in height, with long, pale green, strap-shaped leaves and a loose raceme of twenty to

Gladiolus callianthus (Acidanthera bicolor)

thirty pendent flowers which are white, bell-shaped and about 3 cm (1¼ in) long. It is an elegant plant, worth planting in groups rather than singly.

Gladiolus

A well-known and popular genus of mainly summer-flowering plants in the Iridaceae, although their spikes of irregular hooded flowers are of course completely different from those of the iris and many other members of the family. Nearly all those cultivated are hybrids of a few species from the eastern Cape of South Africa and are winter-dormant; their corms are purchased in spring and planted out when the danger of hard frosts is over. They are then lifted again in the autumn to be stored in a dry, frost-free place. There are a lot of species in the south-west Cape region as well but these are winter-growing, flowering in about January or February in the northern hemisphere, and they are not hardy; they are not generally available and are mainly cultivated by specialist growers who give them cool greenhouse treatment. I have not included these in the list below. In addition to the South African ones there are some European and Asiatic gladioli, which are hardy plants flowering in late spring and suitable for sunny borders; although their flowers are less spectacular than those of the African hybrids they are nevertheless attractive. The corms of these hardy species are obtained and planted in autumn.

Gladioli need sunny, well-drained sites, the corms planted 10–15 cm (4–6 in) deep in soil which has been enriched by the digging in of old, well rotted manure and bonemeal. Once the shoots are through the ground and the plants are growing strongly they need plenty of water for the rest of their development period. The large-flowered hybrids usually need staking, but the other, smaller-flowered types and the species are generally self-supporting.

In the list below I have included a few of the species which can sometimes be found in catalogues, and the major hybrid groups with a selection of cultivars in each of these groups. *Acidanthera* is also included since it is now correctly placed in the genus *Gladiolus*.

G. byzantinus A Mediterranean species up to a metre (3 ft 3 in) tall with showy spikes of bright reddish-purple flowers in late spring. It is a good hardy border plant, increasing well.

G. callianthus (*Acidanthera bicolor*) A delightful tropical African species which can be grown in the same way as the hybrid gladioli, planted out in spring and lifted for the winter. It grows to over a metre (3 ft 3 in) in height and carries in late summer several long-tubed, sweetly scented white flowers with purple blotches in the centres.

G. colvillei A hybrid group derived from South African species, smaller than the large-flowered hybrids at about 30–60 cm (12–24 in) in height. 'The Bride' is one of the best and most easily obtained, a lovely pure white with a green mark in the throat. It can be left in the ground in the milder southern counties and is usually on sale for planting in the autumn.

G. communis A hardy Mediterranean species with spikes of rosy pink flowers, growing to about 50–60 cm (20–24 in) and flowering in May or June.

G. italicus (*G. segetum*) A very common hardy European and Asiatic plant which can be grown successfully in a warm, sunny situation. It is about 50–70 cm (20–28 in) tall, with loose spikes of pink flowers arranged on both sides of the stem, not all facing in one direction.

G. nanus An attractive race of small-flowered hybrids of some South African species, which are fairly hardy and can be left in the ground in areas where the ground does not freeze to a great depth. They grow to about 40–60 cm (16–24 in) in height and have brightly coloured flowers with conspicuous blotches in the throat. 'Amanda Mahy' is a salmon-coloured form, 'Nymph' is white with crimson markings in the throat, 'Spitfire' a bright vermilion, 'Good Luck' a pinkish-red with a darker red centre, and 'Prince Claus' white with red blotches. The corms of these are usually planted in autumn as they start to grow early, but some nurseries still have them in spring.

G. papilio A hardy South African species which flowers in late summer. It grows up to a metre (3 ft 3 in) in height and produces few-flowered spikes of strongly hooded flowers in a pale green and purple mixture. It is very hardy and can be grown in shrub borders, where it may spread into sizeable colonies as its corms produce stolons.

Hybrids There are numerous hybrids available which are used for bedding displays, for cutting or for adding summer colour to mixed borders. Their corms must be lifted and stored for the winter. I have given a small selection of those currently available.

LARGE-FLOWERED
The most vigorous, tallest varieties, up to 1.2 m (4 ft) in height with dense spikes of very large, widely flaring flowers in almost every possible colour.
'Flowersong' – golden yellow with frilled segments, early;
'Deciso' – salmon-pink with a small red patch in the throat;
'Peter Pears' – orange-apricot, early;
'White Friendship' – pure white, early;
'Fidelio' – carmine-purple, late;
'Oscar' – blood-red, mid-season;
'Traderhorn' – scarlet, blotched cream in throat, mid-season.

BUTTERFLY
These have smaller flowers than the above, in less dense spikes up to about a metre (3 ft 3 in) in height. The widely flared flowers are often gaudily coloured, with bright blotches in the throat; they are often offered as mixed collections.
'Melodie' – in shades of salmon and pink with deep red in the throat;
'Camborne' – lilac with a darker patch in the throat;
'Ivanhoe' – yellow, blotched red in the throat;
'Green Woodpecker' – greenish blotched purple.

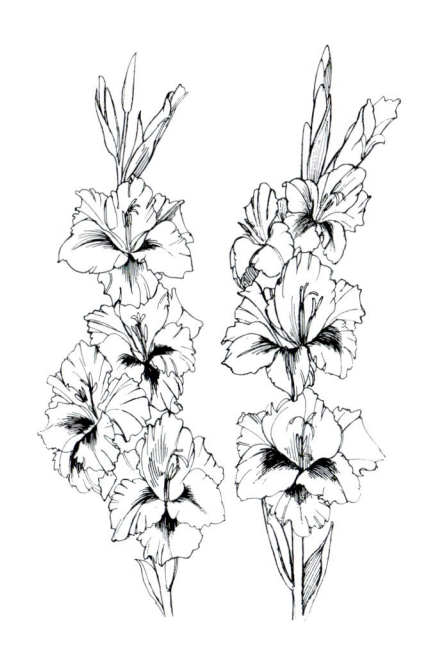

PRIMULINUS
Smaller than the large-flowered types, with looser spikes of flowers which have the upper segment strongly hooded, thus appearing less flaring than in the other types.
'Carioca' – an orange-salmon shade;
'Essex' – purple, blotched white in the throat;
'Yellow Special' – pleasing shade of yellow;
'White City' – pure white.

MINIATURE
These are like small versions of the large-flowered types, with dense spikes of frilled, colourful flowers but only 45–90 cm (18–36 in) tall and with flowers 3–5 cm (1–2 in) across.
'Dancing Doll' – creamy with red throat markings;
'Greenbird' – greenish-yellow with red throat blotches.

Hyacinthus

The ever-popular, marvellously scented hyacinths, so well known for their use indoors in winter, are equally good in the open garden, especially the large-flowered or Cynthella types, which have less dense

Gladiolus Butterfly hybrid

Flowering Bulbs for the Garden

Hyancinthus orientalis cultivars

spikes of flowers. The winter-flowering ones for forcing are sold as 'prepared' bulbs but these are not necessary for outdoor use. They require a well drained, sunny situation, the bulbs being planted about 10–15 cm (4–6 in) deep in autumn. For bedding displays they need to be about 10–15 cm (4–6 in) apart, while in the sunny border, planted in informal groups of about five or six bulbs, they can be slightly closer; used in this way they are excellent for brightening up borders near the house in the spring, and are also ideal for window boxes and tubs on the patio.

All the hyacinth varieties are derived from one species, *H. orientalis*, which is a native of Turkey, south to the Lebanon; it is a smaller plant than its garden counterparts with fewer flowers on the spike.

The following varieties are just a selection of the great many which are available, suitable for outdoor cultivation.

CYNTHELLA
'Sunflower' – a good yellow;
'Debutante' – clear blue;
'Princess Victoria' – rosy pink;
'Snow Queen' – pure white.

LARGE-FLOWERED
'Ostara' – deep blue;
'L'Innocence' – pure white;
'Lady Derby' – pink;
'Jan Bos' – red;
'City of Haarlem' – pale yellow;
'Delft Blue' – rich blue.

Iris magnifica growing wild in Central Asia

IPHEION

A small genus of bulbous plants from South America, distantly related to the onions. Only one species is cultivated to any extent, *I. uniflorum*, and this is an excellent free-flowering plant for the spring garden. It requires a sheltered, semi-shaded spot and does well in humus-rich soil between azaleas and rhododendrons.

I. uniflorum (*Milla uniflora*) Tufts of pale green, narrow leaves which are over-topped by 10–15 cm (4–6 in) stems bearing erect, starry, pale blue flowers about 3–4 cm (up to $1\frac{1}{2}$ in) in diameter. There is a white ('Album') and several richer blue forms of which 'Wisley Blue' and 'Froyle Mill' are good examples. *I. uniflorum* increases well by offset bulbs to form patches, and is good for naturalizing.

IRIS

Apart from the well-known rhizomatous bearded irises, which are not usually stocked by the bulb nurseries since they cannot be dried off and distributed in the dormant state, there are several bulbous groups. These include the popular dwarf reticulatas, the English, Dutch and Spanish irises, and a comparatively little-known but large group, the Junos, which are on the whole more difficult to grow. These three groups are rather different from each other in appearance and cultural requirements, so I will describe them separately.

Reticulata group

These are dwarf plants with netted coats on their bulbs and narrow leaves which are square in section. They are no more than 10–15 cm (4–6 in) in height when in flower and are very suitable for the rock garden, raised beds or alpine house. They all need well-drained soil in full sun, the bulbs giving the best results if planted about 6–8 cm (2¼–3 in) deep. They are obtained in autumn and planted in September or October. Flowering time for all the species and their varieties is in spring, usually March or April but sometimes even earlier in sheltered districts or mild winters.

I. bakeriana From Turkey and Iran, this is different from the rest in having rounded rather than quadrangular leaves. The flowers are pale blue with a dark violet-blue tip to each of the falls, and a strongly blotched area in the centre.

I. danfordiae A small Turkish species, with yellow flowers spotted with green in the centre of the falls. It has the reputation of not flowering well after the first year but deep planting of the bulbs helps, together with feeding with sulphate of potash.

I. histrioides A very attractive species from Turkey which is easy to grow in the open ground, and free flowering. Its large, deep blue flowers emerge almost before the leaves show through. They are made more colourful by a yellow-orange crest on the falls, surrounded by a heavily dark-spotted area. Various named forms have been raised, differing slightly in the depth of colour and amount of spotting. 'Major' has large, very dark flowers; 'Angel's Eye' and 'Lady Beatrix Stanley' are paler, with very prominent blotches on the falls.

I. reticulata The best-known species from Turkey, the Caucasus and Iran, varying widely in colour from nearly blue to deep reddish-purple or white. In cultivation

Iris bucharica

there have been many selections made, and some hybrids with other species. Mostly they are very easily grown and will increase to form floriferous clumps. The following is a selection of those available. The 'common' variety sold as *I. reticulata* is a deep violet with an orange stripe on the falls.
'Cantab' – Cambridge blue with an orange stripe on the falls;
'Harmony' – deep blue with a yellow stripe on the falls;
'Clairette' – pale blue standards and deep blue falls;
'J. S. Dijt' – reddish-purple with an orange stripe of the falls;
'Natasha' – almost white, just faintly tinged with lilac-blue.

I. winogradowii A rarity from the Caucasus with lovely primrose-coloured flowers spotted green, and with an orange stripe on the falls. It is very hardy and increases well but is somewhat expensive at present.

English, Spanish and Dutch irises
Botanically these all belong to the same group, known as the Xiphium irises. They have largish bulbs with papery coats, channelled leaves that are often silvery on the upper side, and tall stems bearing one or more flowers at their apex; if there are two or more they are produced in succession, not together.

These are best known as cut flowers, available by forcing at almost any time of the year. When grown in gardens they flower in early summer and are very good plants for the mixed border, especially the Dutch varieties. The bulbs are obtained in autumn and planted in a well drained, sunny position about 10 cm (4 in) deep.

I. latifolia (*I. xiphioides*) The English iris in fact comes from the Pyrenees. It grows to about 45–60 cm (18–24 in) in height with large purple, blue or white flowers with a central yellow mark on each of the falls, produced in mid summmer. There are named forms but it is usually only possible to obtain mixed collections. It prefers a rich soil which is not too dry in summer.

I. xiphium The Spanish iris grows wild on warm hillsides in Spain and Portugal, and thus likes a sheltered situation which dries out in summer after flowering time in June; a sunny bed at the foot of a south wall is ideal. The flowers are more slender than those of the English iris, and they come in a wide range of colours from white to deep yellow, pale to deep blue, purple and violet. These also are usually offered in mixed colours.

Dutch iris
These are hybrids, mostly between the Spanish iris and a North African species, *I. tingitana*, which is not cultivated very much. They are very popular as cut flowers and are the most successful ones of this group in the garden, making them ideal for planting in groups in mixed borders. The stems are about 50–60 cm (20–24 in) tall, and very stiff so they stand up well to the weather. There is a wide range of colours, and these are usually obtainable in named varieties, such as:
'White Excelsior' – pure white;
'Imperator' and 'Professor Blaauw' – deep blue;
'Bronze Queen' – brownish-bronze;
'Wedgwood' – pale blue;
'Golden Emperor' – bright yellow.

The Dutch irises usually flower in early June.

Juno irises
This group of bulbous irises is on the whole little known in gardens, mainly because the majority of them are difficult to grow even in an alpine house or bulb frame. There are, however, a few which are easy and these can be cultivated in the open garden in a sunny, well-drained site where the bulbs will receive a warm, dryish period after they have died down in summer.

The bulbs of the Juno irises are unusual in having an ordinary-looking bulb but with thick fleshy roots attached to its base; when handling or planting the bulbs these must not be broken off. The bulbs are planted in autumn with the tips at least 7 cm ($2\frac{3}{4}$ in) below the surface.

I. bucharica From Soviet Central Asia, this has stems to about 30–40 cm (12–16 in) tall bearing channelled leaves all the way up and, in the axils of the upper ones, creamy white flowers which have a large yellow area on the falls. These are produced in succession in April or May.

I. graeberiana This Central Asiatic iris is similar in stature to *I. bucharica*, but has pale blue flowers with darker veins on the falls. It is rather uncommon but can usually be found in the specialist catalogues.

I. magnifica Also from the mountains of Central Asia, this superb plant reaches 60 cm (24 in) with several large flowers in palest lilac with an orange patch in the centre of each of the falls. There is a white form, 'Alba', which also has the orange markings. It is one of the best of all the Juno irises and grows well in a sunny situation.

Hermodactylus

There is another curious tuberous-rooted iris in a section of its own, *I. tuberosa*; in fact it is botanically regarded as being distinct from iris and is known as *Hermodactylus tuberosus*. Its finger-like tubers are obtained and planted about 8 cm (3 in) deep in autumn in as hot and sunny a place as possible as they require a good baking in summer and plenty of warmth if they are to flower well in the spring. A situation alongside a warm, sunny wall is best, where you would plant *Iris unguicularis*, nerines and *Amaryllis belladonna*.

I. tuberosa A Mediterranean plant, growing to about 15–25 cm (6–10 in) when in flower, with a solitary flower in a curious translucent greenish colour with purplish-black falls. The leaves are very like those of a reticulata iris, almost square in cross-section. It is sometimes sold as a cut flower in spring.

Ixia

The corn lilies are tender South African cormous plants which are normally treated as winter growing plants for a slightly heated greenhouse, flowering in early spring. Some nurseries, however, offer the dried corms in spring for planting out when the danger of severe frosts has passed, and these will bloom in summer. They require a light soil in a sunny, sheltered situation. There are quite a number of species but usually it is only possible to obtain a mixed collection. The starry flowers, in dense spikes to about 30 cm (12 in) are white, yellow, pink, purple or red, often with a distinct zone of a different colour in the centre.

Ixiolirion

A small genus of one or possibly two species, growing wild in western Asia. The bulbs are planted in autumn in a sunny sheltered place, about 7–8 cm (some 3 in) deep in well-drained soil; a site alongside a south wall is ideal.

I. tataricum (*I. montanum*, *I. pallasii*) grows to about 30–35 cm (12–14 in) in height with wiry stems and narrow leaves. The flowers, several per stem, appear in late spring and are bright blue and funnel shaped, almost like small lilies, facing outwards.

Iris xiphium

Ixiolirion tataricum

Leucojum autumnale

LEUCOJUM

The snowflakes are interesting members of the Amaryllidaceae, with both autumn- and spring-flowering species. Like snowdrops, they have pendent white flowers, with green tips in the spring ones, but are quite distinct in that all six perianth segments are the same size whereas in the snowdrops the three outer ones are over twice the size of the inner ones. The bulbs are planted 5–10 cm (2–4 in) deep depending on size either in autumn or in spring while still in leaf, some nurseries preferring to sell them when green. Since their requirements differ markedly I have mentioned cultivation under each species below.

L. aestivum Flowers in late spring and is the tallest at 30–35 cm (12–14 in). The leaves are daffodil-like and are overtopped by the flower stems which carry up to five white bells with green tips, held on long pedicels. A damp position in sun or semi-shade is best, and it is also good in grass. It grows wild in Europe.

L. autumnale A diminutive autumn-flowering species only 10–15 cm (4–6 in) tall, with very narrow, thread-like leaves and slender stems bearing between one and four small white bells. It is native to the western Mediterranean, and in cultivation thus requires a sunny well-drained position.

L. nicaeense From southern France, this is a delightful spring species with one or two small, widely open bells in pure white on stems not more than 10 cm (4 in) tall; it has narrow, deep green leaves. A sunny position in the rock garden, raised bed or alpine house suits it best.

L. roseum An uncommon early autumn-flowering species, very small and best kept in an alpine house or bulb frame. The solitary, pale pink flowers on stems about 5 cm (2 in) tall are produced just before the thread-like leaves. It is a native of Corsica.

L. vernum Perhaps the most useful garden plant, being robust but dwarf. One or two large, white, green-tipped bells are produced in very early spring almost before the strap-like leaves appear. The stems are only 5–10 cm (2–4 in) to start with, elongating to 15–20 cm (6–8 in) by the end of flowering. There is a version with yellow-tipped flowers known as var. *carpathicum*. *L. vernum* is a European plant, easy to grow in semi-shade in the same conditions as snowdrops.

LILIUM

This large genus provides us with some of the very best summer bulbs, spectacular plants in a good range of colours and shapes for a variety of different garden situations, from full sun to semi-shade, acid or alkaline soils, and in well-drained soil to moist, humus-rich woodland soil.

Lilies have scaly bulbs which are best purchased and planted in autumn, though some nurseries still have them in spring and plantings at this time can be quite successful. When in growth they can be divided into two groups on the basis of whether or not they have roots growing out of the stem just above the bulb; in the descriptions below they are noted as being stem rooting or not. The stem rooters need to be planted deeper so that these extra feeding roots have plenty of soil in which to develop. Most of the popular lilies have stem roots, and their bulbs should be planted 6–8 cm (2¼–3 in) deep if fairly small or 10–20 cm (4–8 in) for those with very large bulbs. Non stem-rooting bulbs need only 6–10 cm (2¼–4 in) depending on size, and *L. candidum* should be even shallower, with about 1 cm (less than ½ in) of soil above the tip of the bulb.

The soil should, for nearly all lilies, be well-drained and have a good humus content, preferably of leafmould or old rotted compost or manure rather than peat. Gritty sand should be mixed in if the drainage is poor. The individual descriptions indicate which varieties are lime tolerant, and which sort of situation is best. They can be grown in borders of other perennial plants or in shrub borders, or in containers for the patio or terrace. Growing lilies in pots can be very successful as conditions can be controlled quite accurately; deep pots are necessary, especially for the stem rooters, and obviously with vigorous species and varieties the nutrients will soon be used up so it is essential to feed with an all-round fertilizer through the summer, such as National Growmore or tomato fertilizer.

For convenience I have placed the lilies into three informal groups based on their overall flower shape, though in the case of some hybrids this is not altogether clearcut. The first, group A, are of the pendent 'turkscap' type with the perianth segments sharply reflexed or curled right back; group B contains the large trumpet-shaped ones, often heavily fragrant with the flowers facing outwards; and group C, which is the most varied, includes those with upright or outward-facing, flattish, saucer-shaped or bowl-shaped flowers, sometimes, as in the case of the large-flowered hybrids of *L. auratum*, with reflexed tips to the segments. Most lilies flower in July or August; I have commented if they are particularly early or late.

Group A

Pendent-flowered lilies, mostly of the turkscap-type with their flower segments reflexed or rolled back. A few are pendent, with the tips only slightly recurved (or not recurved at all, as in *L. mackliniae*).

L. amabile From Korea, and less than a metre (3 ft 3 in) tall, with many narrow, grassy leaves and five to ten small turkscap flowers in deep red, spotted black. Var. *luteum* has yellow flowers. Stem rooting. Needs good drainage in sun, acid or alkaline soil.

L. canadense A graceful North American lily up to a metre (3 ft 3 in) tall with whorls of leaves and five to fifteen yellow bells with the segments slightly curved outwards. There are plain or dark-spotted forms, and orange or red. Not stem rooting. Needs a moist, humus-rich, acid soil in semi-shade.

L. carniolicum is 40–60 cm (16–24 in) tall, with narrow leaves and red turkscap flowers. Var. *albanicum* is yellow. It is a Balkan species, stem rooting, and likes sharp drainage in full sun, preferably on alkaline soils. Rather rare.

L. cernuum, a rare species from Korea, grows only 30–60 cm (12–24 in) in height with a few pinkish-purple, dark-spotted turkscap flowers on slender, narrowly leafy stems. It requires well-drained soil, acid or alkaline. Stem rooting.

L. chalcedonicum A Greek species growing to about a metre (3 ft 3 in) or more in height, with grey-green leaves held close to the stem and between one and six brilliant, waxy red turkscap flowers. It prefers a well-drained, sunny situation and is best on alkaline soils. Not stem-rooting.

L. × testaceum is a hybrid of this and *L. candidum* which has lovely soft apricot-coloured turkscap flowers with bright orange stamens.

L. davidii from eastern Asia grows up to 1.5 m (5 ft) with very many long, narrow leaves and up to twenty large turkscap flowers in bright orange, spotted darker towards the centre. Var. *willmottiae* is a particularly vigorous form. Stem rooting. The best site is in semi-shade in acid or alkaline soil that has been enriched with leafmould.

L. duchartrei is a species from China, unusual in that its bulbs produce stolons and eventually form patches. It has slender stems to 1.2 m (4 ft), carrying scattered leaves and several small, scented, turkscap flowers with a white ground colour spotted with purple. Stem rooting. It will grow in semi-shade in acid or alkaline soils if there is plenty of humus present.

L. hansonii Like the martagon lily, this Korean species has its leaves in whorls on the 1–1.5 m (3 ft 3 in–5 ft) stems, but has up to ten deep yellow turkscap flowers spotted with brown. Stem rooting. It likes leafmould-rich soil, acid or alkaline, in semi-shade.

L. henryi A very vigorous Chinese species with tough stems bearing scattered broad leaves, reaching 2 m (6 ft 6 in) or more when growing well. The large orange turkscap flowers are carried on long stalks well away from the stem and have curious raised protections all over the centre. Stem rooting. A very easy lily for a semi-shaded site in soil rich in leafmould, preferably neutral or alkaline.

L. mackliniae A beautiful rarity from Burma which is not a turkscap type but does have pendulous flowers. They are white, flushed with pinkish-purple, one to five of them carried on stems up to 80 cm (32 in) tall. Stem rooting. It needs a cool, humid situation in soil rich in peat or leafmould, and is best in the higher rainfall areas of the north and west.

L. martagon The European and Asiatic martagon lily is an old favourite in gardens, distinctive with its whorls of leaves and raceme of small pinkish turkscap flowers. It is one of the first to flower in early summer. When growing vigorously it can have up to fifty flowers on stems up to 1.5 m (5 ft) tall. There are various colour forms and it is worth trying to get a good rich pinkish-purple, the white 'Album', or one of the very dark wine-coloured varieties, *cattaniae* or *dalmaticum*. It is a stem-rooting lily which prefers semi-shade in acid or alkaline soils to which leafmould has been added.

Lilium martagon has been crossed with the yellow *L. hansonii* to produce a race of early flowering hybrids which are vigorous, disease-resistant plants suitable for any reasonably well-drained position in partial shade, such as a shrub border. The Backhouse hybrids vary widely in colour from yellow to cream to buff or pinkish, dark-spotted inside. 'Mrs R.O. Backhouse' is one of these, in orange-yellow flushed with pink; 'Marhan' is orange-yellow spotted with brown; 'Jacques S. Dijt' has creamy flowers spotted purple; × *dalhansonii* is a deep maroon with an orange centre.

L. maximowiczii (*L. leichtlinii* var. *maximowiczii*) An eastern Asiatic species which can grow to 2 m (6 ft 6 in), the stems densely clothed with many narrow leaves and several large orange, black-spotted, turkscap flowers. It is stem rooting and is best in semi-shade in a humus-rich, non-alkaline soil.

L. monadelphum This beautiful Caucasian species is uncommon but well worth seeking. Its strong stems to 1.5 m (5 ft) are densely clad in rather broad leaves and carry in early summer several large, pale yellow turkscap flowers, dark-spotted within. It is a stem-rooting lily suitable for leafmould-rich soil in semi-shade, and seems to do particularly well on alkaline soils though I have seen good clumps among rhododendrons.

Lilium szovitsianum is very like this and from a garden point of view is of similar value.

Lilium henryi

L. pardalinum One of the several North American lilies which have tall stems up to 2 m (6 ft 6 in) in height, with whorled leaves and large turkscap flowers, in this case a pale orange-red spotted internally with dark brownish-red and with darker red tips to the segments. It is not a stem-rooting type and prefers damp, humus-rich soils with the bulbs planted quite shallowly, not more than 10 cm (4 in) deep. It is lime tolerant only if the soil is rich in humus.

Lilium pardalinum, the panther or leopard lily, is one of the parents of a range of American hybrids, including the famous Bellingham hybrids, which range in colour from deep orange to yellow, strongly spotted red or purple-red. 'Shuksan' is one of these, in orange shaded and spotted with red. They are vigorous, hardy plants suitable for a damp, semi-shaded situation.

Lilium superbum is of the same general appearance and is, as its name suggests, an excellent plant when growing well, with thirty or forty flowers.

L. pomponium A rarity from the mountains of southern France with 50–65 cm (20–26 in) stems carrying narrow leaves and brilliant red turkscap flowers which have a sealing-wax texture. It needs warm, sunny conditions with good drainage, preferably on alkaline soil. Stem rooting.

L. pumilum (*L. tenuifolium*) An easily cultivated little lily of delicate appearance from eastern Asia. It grows to only 45–60 cm (18–24 in) with many narrow leaves and several scarlet turkscap flowers which are pleasantly fragrant. There is a yellow-orange form known as 'Golden Gleam'. It is stem rooting and likes good drainage in a sunny situation. Seeds are produced freely, and these will make flowering sized bulbs in only one or two years.

L. pyrenaicum This Pyrenean species is one of the easiest of lilies, an old favourite in cottage gardens. It forms clumps of bulbs when growing well, with stems up to a metre tall densely clothed with leaves and carrying in May or June several turkscaps which are spotted and streaked black inside. It is stem rooting, and it will grow in sun or semi-shade in reasonably well-drained soil, acid or alkaline though the latter is preferred.

L. speciosum A Japanese species, notable for its large, fragrant flowers produced in the autumn. The wiry stems to a metre (3 ft 3 in) or more in height have tough broad leaves and several large flowers which are turkscap in shape but much larger than most. They are white, flushed with pink and covered in the centre with red, hair-like projections. Var. *album* is completely white and var. *rubrum* is suffused with crimson. It is a stem-rooting lily which prefers cool, humid but well-drained growing conditions with plenty of humus in the soil; it is liable to be caught by early autumn frosts in cold districts so a sheltered spot in semi-shade is necessary.

Lilium speciosum has been selected and hybridized, sometimes with *L. auratum*, to produce a whole range of large, colourful, late-flowering lilies, for example 'Uchida' (deep crimson-red), 'Ellabee' (white), 'Lucie Wilson' (pink). Some of the lilies in the group known as Oriental hybrids are also like large turkscaps, though others have flatter flowers more like those of *L. auratum* and are mentioned below in our group C. Oriental hybrids with recurved segments like those of *L. speciosum* include 'Black Beauty', 'Jamboree Strain', 'Bonfire' and 'Journey's End', all of which are various shades of rich crimson or maroon, edged with white.

L. tigrinum This old favourite, the Chinese or Japanese tiger lily, is a late-flowering one, usually not flowering before August. It has several large orange turkscap flowers spotted black inside, carried on leafy stems to 2 m (6 ft 6 in) high. It is a stem-rooting type which likes a sheltered position in sun – it was a good cottage garden plant in times gone by. There is an extra vigorous form known as var. *fortunei*, and a good one with large, deep orange-red flowers known as 'Splendens'. Var. *flaviflorum* has pale yellow flowers. There is even a double form, 'Flore Pleno', which though unusual is not exactly beautiful!

Many hybrids owe at least part of their pedigree to *L. tigrinum*.

Lily hybrids with turkscap-shaped flowers In addition to the species there are many hybrids with pendent turkscap flowers, mostly excellent hardy, easily cultivated lilies which are stem rooting and lime tolerant. They like sunny positions but with a little shade at midday if possible, as some colours fade a little in very bright sunlight. The following is just a small selection of the enormous range:

Lilium regale

'Bright Star' – white with a yellow band on each segment giving a star-like centre;
'Carnival Strain' – large pendent flowers with reflexing segments in yellow, apricot and white;
'Citronella' – yellow, spotted black;
'Fiesta Hybrids' – yellow, orange or red, spotted darker;
'Lady Bowes-Lyon' – deep red, spotted black;
'Pan' – white;
'Viking' – orange-red.

GROUP B
Trumpet-shaped lilies with outward-facing flowers, mostly much larger than in group A.

L. formosanum From Taiwan (Formosa), this has 15 cm (6 in) long white, fragrant trumpets on narrowly leafy stems a metre (3 ft 3 in) or more tall. It is too tender for outdoors, but can be grown in a cool greenhouse in tubs and then stood out on a patio when in flower. Seeds sown at the beginning of the year in a heated greenhouse can produce flowering bulbs late in the same year. It is stem rooting. Var. *pricei* is a much hardier, dwarf form which flowers earlier and can be grown in a semi-shaded site rich in humus.

L. longiflorum The Easter lily, can also be grown in pots and is even quicker to reach flowering size from seed. Its elegant white trumpets are up to 20 cm (8 in) long. Unfortunately it is not at all hardy.

L. regale One of the most famous lilies of all, this beautiful Chinese species is a very easily cultivated plant, reaching flowering in only two or three years from seed. Its leafy stems grow to 1–2 m (3 ft 3 in–6 ft 6 in) in height, with large white trumpets stained with purple on the outside and suffused yellow in the throat. Twenty or more flowers may be produced in vigorous specimens. It is a stem-rooting type which can be grown on acid or alkaline soils which have had leafmould or peat worked in well; sun or semi-shaded situations are equally successful.

Lilium 'Enchantment'

Trumpet hybrids There are a great many hybrid lilies with trumpet-shaped flowers, some of which are rather wide open because of mixed parentage with the turkscap-shaped *L. henryi* (e.g. the Aurelian hybrids). They are mostly very tall, vigorous plants 1–2 m (3 ft 3 in–6 ft 6 in) in height and are stem rooters, tolerant of acid or alkaline conditions provided that there is good drainage with a good humus content to the soil. They are valuable for planting in the mixed border or for use in tubs on the patio. The following are good, hardy, easily cultivated trumpet lilies:
'African Queen' – a strain varying from apricot to orange-yellow;
'Aurelian Hybrids' – very variable in colour and shape;
'Golden Splendour' – deep gold, flushed purple-bronze outside;
'Green Dragon' – yellowish-green;
'Pink Pearl' – pink with a darker purplish stain outside;
'Pink Perfection' – soft pink in various shades.

GROUP C
Flattish or very wide open bowl- or saucer-shaped flowers, upward- or outward-facing, sometimes with reflexing tips.

L. auratum A late summer- or autumn-flowering lily with wiry stems clothed with broad leaves, reaching to 1–2 m (3 ft 3 in–6 ft 6 in) in height. The several saucer-shaped flowers can be up to 30 cm (12 in) across, and are normally white spotted with yellow and with a yellow band along the centre of each segment, hence the name golden rayed lily in its native Japan. Var. *rubrum* has a red stripe on each segment.

There are some colourful cultivars, and many hybrids known as Oriental Hybrids. These have *L. speciosum* as the other parent, so in some of them there is a tendency to the turkscap shape of flower inherited from the latter; these are mentioned under group A. Those with flowers more like *L. auratum* in shape include 'Imperial Gold' – white with a yellow band; 'Imperial

Silver' – white spotted red; 'Red Band Hybrids' – crimson in varying shades; 'Star Gazer' – deep crimson.

Lilium auratum and the Oriental Hybrids are stem-rooting lilies and are intolerant of lime in the soil. They require a semi-shaded position with plenty of leafmould, and the drainage must be good.

L. candidum Probably the oldest lily in cultivation, the Mediterranean madonna lily differs from most in having leaves through the winter. The bulbs are planted in August only just beneath the surface in a warm, sunny situation, preferably on alkaline or neutral soils. It is not stem rooting. The flower stems reach to 1.5 m (5 ft) in June or July and carry several wide open, pure white flowers which are deliciously fragrant.

L. concolor A small species from China which likes a well-drained, sunny position with a good humus content. Its stems reach only 80 cm (32 in) at most, topped by upward-facing, flattish flowers in bright red, sometimes spotted darker and sometimes wholly yellow. It is stem rooting.

L. croceum (*L. bulbiferum* var. *croceum*) The orange lily, a European species that can reach 1.5 m (5 ft), with densely leafy stems and at the apex a cluster of erect, bowl-like flowers in bright orange. It is a stem-rooting type, fairly easy to grow in slight shade in acid or alkaline soil which is reasonably well drained.

L. dauricum This eastern Asiatic species is fairly dwarf at 30–60 cm (12–24 in), bearing upright, bowl-shaped flowers in red, spotted darker. It is stem rooting and will grow best in well-drained acid or neutral soil, in a sunny position.

Hybrids with upright or outward-facing flat or bowl-shaped flowers There are a great many hybrids with this type of flower, very popular at present as they are easy to grow in the open garden or in tubs, and are often sold as cut flowers. They are stem-rooting lilies requiring reasonably well drained, acid or alkaline soil in sun or semi-shade. The following is but a very small selection to show the range of colours available; new ones are being introduced every year.

'Brandywine' – outward-facing, orange spotted blackish inside;
'Chinook' – upright, pale apricot;
'Connecticut King' – upright, bright clear yellow, unspotted;
'Corsage' – outward-facing, cream shading to pink at tips, spotted purple;
'Destiny' – upright, yellow, spotted brownish-red;
'Enchantment' – upright, orange, spotted black;
'Fire King' – outward-facing, orange-red, spotted;
'Firecracker' – upright, deep red;
'Pink Beauty' – outward-facing, pink, darker towards the centre;
'Pirate' – upright, orange-red;
'Sterling Star' – upright, white, prominently spotted brown;
'Yellow Star' – outward-facing, yellow, spotted brown.

These are called Asiatic hybrids, some of them belonging to the famous 'Mid Century' group.

MERENDERA

This smallish genus is related to the colchicum, and has similar upright, goblet-

Merendera montana

shaped flowers but instead of their having a long tube the perianth segments are separated all the way down. Only one species is cultivated to any extent, and even this is fairly uncommon.

M. montana (*M. bulbocodium*) An autumn-flowering species with large, rosy-lilac flowers about 5 cm (2 in) across, almost resting on the ground and produced before the rosette of narrow leaves appears. It is a native of the Pyrenees. In cultivation it needs a sunny, well-drained position and is suitable for a rock garden, the bulbs being planted in autumn about 5 cm (2 in) deep.

Moraea

A South African genus in the Iridaceae and looking very similar to irises in their flower shape. Most of them are not frost hardy, but a few from the Eastern Cape can be grown outside in Britain, and make attractive border plants for a position which is sunny but does not dry out too much in summer. They are usually obtainable as growing plants in pots through nurseries specializing in perennials rather than as dried bulbs, as the corms do not take to being dried out.

M. spathulata (*M. spathacea*) forms clumps of long, narrow, very tough leaves, and in summer flower stems to about 1 m (3 ft 3 in) carrying a succession of yellow flowers from the tight bracts. Each flower is about 6–8 cm ($2\frac{1}{4}$–3 in) across, flattish and bearing darker markings towards the base of the three large outer segments. It flowers in early to midsummer. *M. moggii* and *M. huttonii* are also in cultivation and are rather similar in overall appearance.

Muscari

The grape hyacinths are a valuable group of spring-flowering bulbs, perhaps somewhat scorned at times because of one species, *M. neglectum*, which can be very weedy. They are mostly easy to grow in sun or semi-shade, the bulbs being planted in autumn about 5–7 cm (2–$2\frac{3}{4}$ in) deep. With their dense spikes of small blue flowers several of the common species are very suitable for naturalizing between and beneath shrubs.

M. armeniacum A very free-flowering Turkish species, ideal for mass planting under shrubs to produce a blue haze. It has long racemes of deep purplish-blue flowers on 15–20 cm (6–8 in) stems. There is a double form, 'Blue Spike', which is especially showy and suitable for bedding schemes.

M. azureum (*Hyacinthus azureus*) A dwarf Turkish species only 8–12 cm (3–5 in) in height, with short, dense spikes of bright blue flowers which differ from most grape hyacinths in being bell-shaped without a constricted mouth. It is ideal for a rock garden. There is a white form, 'Album'.

M. botryoides From the Balkans, this has dense spikes of almost spherical, rich blue flowers, each with a very constricted mouth with a white rim. Like its white form, 'Album', it is a good rock garden plant, not spreading too rapidly.

M. comosum The tassel hyacinth, so called because the long racemes have a tassel-like cluster of bright blue, sterile flowers at the apex. The stems are 15–30 cm (6–12 in) in height, with spaced-out, fertile flowers of brownish-green. 'Plumosum' (or 'Monstrosum') is a curious form in which all the flowers are sterile and bluish-mauve. It is easily cultivated in full sun.

M. macrocarpum A striking species with a delicious fruity scent, but best cultivated in an alpine house or bulb frame as its bulbs require a hot, dry period in summer. It is about 20–25 cm (8–10 in) in height, with broad, greyish leaves and fairly dense spikes of nodding, bright yellow flowers with a brown rim around the mouth; the upper sterile flowers are purplish. It is a native of Mediterranean Turkey and nearby islands.

M. muscarimi (*M. moschatum*) This Turkish species is similar in overall appearance

Flowering Bulbs for the Garden

Moraea huttonii

to *M. macrocarpum* but has greyish-white or slightly bluish flowers with a very strong musk scent. It requires alpine house or bulb frame cultivation.

M. neglectum (*M. racemosum*) This is the most common species both in the wild, in Europe and western Asia, and in gardens.

It has dense, 10–20 cm (4–8 in) spikes of fragrant, blackish-blue flowers with a white rim around the constricted mouth. It spreads very freely by seeds and offset bulbs and is probably best kept out of the rock garden, being more suitable for naturalizing beneath shrubs or in grass.

M. tubergenianum One of the more spectacular species in Oxford and Cambridge colours, the 10–20 cm (4–8 in) stems having both deep blue and pale flowers on the same spike, which is very densely flowered. It originated from northern Iran and is a very good spring bulb for planting on the rock garden.

Narcissus

The daffodils and narcissus need little introduction and are some of our best spring bulbs. Most of those seen in gardens are hybrids, of which there are hundreds varying from the large trumpet types to the small-cupped pheasant's eye and the

Muscari armeniacum

graceful modern Cyclamineus and Triandrus hybrids with their swept-back corolla. There are also quite a number of species, which range from dwarf plants of a few centimetres up to normal sized daffodils, and several of these, too, make good garden plants, though some of the small ones flower too early in the year to be very successful outside and are best grown in an alpine house or bulb frame.

Narcissus bulbs are purchased in autumn and planted from 5–15 cm (2–6 in) deep, depending upon the size of the bulb – the small species at the shallow end of the scale and the vigorous hybrids much deeper. All narcissus will do best in sunny situations in well-drained soil, but some will take slight shade such as that provided by apple trees, and daffodils in grass under fruit trees are a charming sight. Waterlogged soils are not suitable, but in dampish situations the hybrids of *N. cyclamineus* and *N. poeticus* varieties are worth trying. When they are grown in grass it is worth remembering that you cannot cut the grass soon after flowering; it is best to leave mowing until their foliage has turned yellow; it has been shown that cutting can begin as soon as six weeks after the last flower has faded without damaging the performance of the bulbs in subsequent years. The bulb leaves should not be tied up in knots as one occasionally sees in 'tidy' gardens, for this too is harmful and weakens the bulbs.

N. asturiensis (*N. minimus*) This is the smallest of the trumpet daffodil species, from northern Spain. It is under 10 cm (4 in) tall, with narrow, grey leaves and perfect miniature trumpet flowers in deep yellow only 2 cm (less than 1 in) long. It flowers in early spring and is best in a well-drained spot on a raised bed or rock garden, or in the alpine house.

N. bulbocodium The hoop petticoat daffodil is quite different from other species (except its relative *N. cantabricus*) in having a wide, funnel-shaped corona and very narrow perianth segments (corolla). It is very variable over its wide range in Spain, Portugal and North Africa, from 5–15 cm

Narcissus cyclamineus

(2–6 in) tall and with flower colour from pale sulphur yellow to deep buttercup; the leaves are very narrow and almost thread-like. Flowering very early, this is best in a sunny rock garden, bulb frame or alpine house, though it will sometimes settle in a peat garden if not too shady, or in turf if it is made up of fine grasses. Var. *citrinus* has primrose-coloured flowers; var. *obesus* is deep yellow with leaves which tend to coil on the ground; var. *nivalis* (*N. nivalis*) is a tiny plant only about 5 cm (2 in) in height; subsp. *romieuxii* has very pale sulphur or lemon flowers in winter and is best kept in an alpine house or frame.

N. canaliculatus A small tazetta-type narcissus from the Mediterranean region, about 20 cm (8 in) tall with up to seven flowers in a head, white with a small yellow cup and sweetly scented. It needs a hot, sunny position if it is to flower reliably each year.

N. cantabricus This is like a white version of *N. bulbocodium*, flowering very early – often in late winter. It is a very delicate plant which is easily spoiled by inclement weather, so is best kept in an alpine house or bulb frame. *N. clusii* is a variant of this.

N. cyclamineus A lovely, distinct little species from Spain and Portugal with bright green, rather than greyish, leaves, with flower stems to about 15 cm (6 in) in height carrying solitary yellow flowers which have a long trumpet and swept-back perianth segments, giving it the 'cyclamen' look. It is best grown in a moist spot which dries out to some extent in summer, such as a peat garden or in short turf, but it is also a fine plant for a pocket on the rock garden which is not too hot and sunbaked.

Narcissus cyclamineus has been crossed with various other daffodils to give us a range of lovely taller garden plants known as the Cyclamineus hybrids, the most famous of which is the deep yellow early 'February Gold', which is about 30 cm (12 in) tall. Other good varieties are 'Tête-à-Tête', a stocky one only 15 cm (6 in) tall, with deep yellow flowers, often two per stem; 'Jack Snipe', about 20 cm (8 in) with white perianth and a yellow cup; 'Jumblie', with stems about 25 cm (10 in) tall carrying two to three flowers in deep yellow; and 'Jenny', a graceful flower with a white, swept-back perianth and a long, creamy trumpet, about 30 cm (12 in) tall. These hybrids are easily cultivated in sun or slight shade, and the stronger ones will do well in grass, especially 'February Gold'.

N. jonquilla The jonquil is popular as a winter cut flower, especially for its delicious fragrance. The wild form from Spain and Portugal is about 30 cm (12 in) tall with long, narrow deep green leaves and up to five bright yellow, flattish flowers which are about 2–3 cm (about 1 in) across with a smallish cup and a long perianth tube. There is a double form, also very fragrant.

In addition to the wild species there are some hybrids derived from it bearing the characteristic of several smallish flowers per stem. 'Lintie' is a small one, about 20 cm (8 in) tall with two or three fragrant flowers with a yellow perianth and an orange-rimmed cup; 'Waterperry' is white with an apricot cup, about 25 cm (10 in) tall; 'Trevithian' is taller, about 30–35 cm (12–14 in), and has two or three fragrant flowers which are pale yellow throughout.

N. juncifolius This small species from south-west Europe is like a miniature jonquil, up to 15 cm (6 in) tall with slender, cylindrical green leaves and several flattish, deep yellow flowers only 2 cm (less than 1 in) across; the cup is shallow and rather frilly at the edges. It can be grown in a sunny, well-drained rock garden and is also very suitable for an alpine house. *N. rupicola* is rather similar in flower shape but has only one flower per stem, and grey leaves. *N. scaberulus* is a smaller version of *N. rupicola*, with flowers only 1 cm ($\frac{1}{2}$ in) across.

N. poeticus The very late-flowering poet's narcissus is well known in gardens in its form called pheasant's eye. The 30–45 cm (12–18 in) stems carry solitary, fragrant flowers in pure white or cream with a very shallow orange or red corona in the centre, more like a crinkled disc than a cup in some of the wild forms. In its native mountains of southern Europe it often grows in moist meadows, and in consequence it is very suitable for planting in grass or a damp but sunny spot in the garden. There are some garden forms with much larger flowers, for example 'Cantabile', with perfect white flowers with a red-rimmed cup which is green in the centre, and 'Actaea', nearly 10 cm (4 in) in diameter, also with a red-margined cup. They are excellent garden plants.

There are also hybrids between *N. poeticus* and *N. tazetta* known as the 'Poetaz' group, the best of which is probably 'Geranium'. This has several scented, flattish white flowers with shallow orange cups, carried on 35–40 cm (14–16 in) stems. Unlike *N. tazetta* it is an easy plant to grow and flower even in cold areas, and will do well in grass; *N. tazetta* is a poor doer and requires a warm, sheltered situation.

N. pseudonarcissus This is the wild originator of many of the large hybrid trumpet daffodils, a common plant of western Europe and occurring in Britain as well, where it is known as the lent lily. It is extremely variable in size, from stocky little forms of only 10 cm (4 in) up to 'normal' sized daffodils, in colours from pure white to pale to deep yellow, or sometimes bicoloured with a white corolla and yellow trumpet. Names have been given to many of the variants. Subsp. *obvallaris* is the Tenby daffodil, naturalized in Wales, which has deep yellow flowers, fairly uniform in colour, on 15 cm (6 in) stems; subsp. *alpestris* (*N. moschatus*) from the Pyrenees has nodding white flowers; the Spanish subsp. *abscissus* has very straight yellow trumpets, cut across squarely at the mouth rather than flared out and crinkled; subsp. *nobilis*, also from Spain, has large bicoloured flowers on very short stems.

N. lobularis, with nodding, pale primrose flowers, is very similar in overall appearance and is probably another variant; it is a good early-flowering dwarf daffodil. *N. pseudonarcissus* subsp. *pallidiflorus* is also, as its name suggests, a pale one in a delicate soft yellow. Smaller than all of these is *N. nanus*, only 10 cm (4 in) tall, with bicoloured flowers having a creamy yellow corolla and deeper yellow trumpet.

All these wild forms of the daffodil are good garden plants suitable for borders, rock gardens in the case of the smaller ones, and for naturalizing in grass.

The large daffodil hybrids such as 'King Alfred' are derived from these, and are the backbone of spring garden displays. They come in a great range of colours and sizes, from pure white as in 'Cantatrice' and 'Vigil', to the deep yellows of 'Unsurpassable' and 'Golden Harvest'. Cream and yellow bicolors include 'Foresight' and 'Queen of Bicolors', and there is an ever-increasing number of the pink trumpet varieties which at present tend to be rather expensive.

N. tazetta The wild cluster-headed Mediterranean tazetta is not a good garden plant for most areas as its bulbs require a sun-baking in summer if they are to flower well, and the early flowers and leaves can be damaged by serious frosts. It has up to ten, or even more, small, very fragrant flowers, usually white with a yellow cup but there are variations with wholly yellow flowers. The pure white *N. papyraceus* (the paper white narcissus) is related, and is also too tender for outdoor cultivation in most of the country.

'Soleil d'Or' is a well known variety much used as a cut flower in winter. The double 'Cheerfulness' and 'Yellow Cheerfulness' are possibly derived from *N. tazetta*, and these can be cultivated successfully in the open garden though they are also very popular for forcing for their early fragrant blooms.

N. triandrus The angel's tears narcissus from Spain is a most attractive dwarf one, about 15–20 cm (6–8 in) tall with two to five nodding flowers with sharply reflexed perianth segments. The usual form has creamy-white flowers and is often sold as 'Albus', but there is a yellow variation as well, var. *concolor*. It is easy to grow in a rock garden, or in grass if not too coarse, or in the alpine house.

Hybrids of *N. triandrus* are mostly taller than the wild species at 20–35 cm (8–10 in), and have several larger flowers per stem. They are lovely, and make excellent garden plants for sunny, well-drained positions. They mostly have slightly reflexed corolla segments inherited from *N. triandrus*. Popular varieties include 'Tresamble' and 'Thalia', both white, 'Liberty Bells' in pale yellow, and 'April Tears', a deeper yellow and shorter than most at about 15–20 cm (6–8 in).

Narcissus poeticus hybrid

N. watieri This charming little North African species is best kept in the alpine house or bulb frame as its bulbs need a warm, dry period in summer. It has solitary, flat, white flowers with a very shallow cup on stems about 10 cm (4 in) tall, and has very grey leaves.

Hybrids In addition to those hybrids mentioned above under the species from which they are derived there are many that are intermediate between their parents and are best dealt with separately. The most important groups are those with deep cup-shaped coronas, in between the trumpet daffodils and the small-cupped narcissi such as *N. poeticus* and *N. tazetta*; these hybrids are classified by the Royal Horticultural Society as 'Large Cupped' when the cup is more than one-third the length of the perianth segments, and 'Small Cupped' when it is less than one-third as long. Examples of the large-cupped types are 'Passionale', white with a pink cup, 'Kilworth', white with an orange-red cup, 'Carlton', wholly yellow, and 'Ice Follies', in pure white with a lemon cup which ages to white. Small-cupped varieties include 'Verger', with white perianth and a pale yellow cup edged orange, 'Polar Ice', a wholly white one, and 'Birma', with yellow perianth and a scarlet cup.

In addition to these there are double varieties such as 'Telamonius Plenus' ('Van Sion'), which is the robust double yellow daffodil of old, 'White Marvel', with several double white flowers on each stem, and 'Irene Copeland' with white and yellow segments mixed in a tightly double flower.

A new line in narcissus breeding is the collar or split corona daffodil, sometimes called orchid flowering. In these the trumpet is split and pressed back against the perianth, making a flattish flower with two layers of 'petals'. 'Baccarat' is a colourful one, with yellow perianth and a flat orange collar inside it; 'Cassata' has a white perianth and yellow collar. They are not to everyone's liking, having lost the classic shape of the daffodil and narcissus, but are certainly unusual.

NECTAROSCORDUM

A small genus of only three or four species, closely related to the onion family and having the same characteristic smell when the leaves or bulbs are damaged. The two in cultivation are vigorous plants, very easy to grow in the mixed perennial border or suitable for naturalizing between shrubs or in grass. The bulbs should be planted in autumn about 10 cm (4 in) deep.

N. siculum (*N. dioscoridis*) This southern European species grows to about 1 m (3 ft 3in) in height, with long, strongly keeled leaves and tough, wiry stems which carry umbels of flowers in May or June; these are pendent, held on long stalks and are bell-shaped in green and purple, about 2.5 cm (1 in) long.

N. ectaroscordum bulgaricum from Bulgaria and Turkey, this is a similar species except for its whitish flowers tinged with green.

Both of these have attractive seed heads suitable for drying for the winter, the flower stalks turning upright as they mature to hold the capsules erect.

NERINE

The autumn-flowering nerines are South African in origin and only one of them, *N. bowdenii*, is reliably hardy in Britain. The bulbs can be planted in late summer to early autumn, or in the spring; they should

Nerine bowdenii

be planted in well-drained soil in a warm, sunny situation such as at the foot of a south-facing wall, with the neck of the bulbs covered by about 5 cm (2 in) of soil. A dressing of bonemeal or a potash-rich fertilizer (such as is given to tomatoes) in spring may encourage flowering.

N. bowdenii This is about 40–60 cm (16–24 in) in height when in flower in September to November. Its flower stems emerge before the leaves and carry large umbels of up to ten glistening pink flowers with narrow, wavy segments. The strap-like geeen leaves appear soon after and remain in growth until the following summer, when they die away. At this stage as much sun as possible should be allowed to fall on the resting bulbs to encourage bud formation, so clear away any encroaching neighbouring plants. 'Fenwick's Variety' or 'Mark Fenwick' is a more vigorous plant, up to 1 cm (3 ft 3 in) tall, with deeper-coloured flowers. There is also a white form, 'Alba', which is rather rare in cultivation; some new hybrids are being raised which are fairly hardy.

NOMOCHARIS

These are lovely Chinese relatives of lilies, but are much more difficult to grow except in cool, humid districts such as the north and west. Their bulbs and leafy stems, which produce additional roots just above the bulb, are very similar to those of lilies, but the flattish or saucer-shaped flowers, which are nodding or facing outwards, do look rather different. The perianth segments have swollen areas or crests near the base and the colours are mostly in the white to pink or reddish range, often spotted and blotched darker, or with a purple 'eye'.

In cultivation they need cool conditions, with plenty of moisture available through their growing season; a semi-shaded site with a humus-rich soil suits them best. Only a few species are in cultivation, and these are rather rare.

N. aperta Can grow up to 1 m (3 ft 3 in) in height, but usually much less in cultivation, with pairs of leaves on the stem and up to six nodding, saucer-like flowers about 8–10 cm (5–6 in) across; these are pale pink, blotched deep purple, with a dark purple eye in the centre.

N. mairei Has whorls of leaves, not pairs, on the 60–70 cm (24–28 in) stems, and several flattish flowers about 10 cm (4 in) across; the inner segments are provided with a fringe around the margins. The ground colour is white, strongly blotched reddish-purple all over the segments, and there is an eye of deep red-purple.

N. pardanthina This also has whorls of leaves and several flattish flowers but, unlike *N. mairei*, no frilled margins to the segments. The ground colour is pink and

Nomocharis pardanthina

Ornithogalum thyrsoides

there are purple spots, but only towards the base of the segments; it too has a purple eye in the centre.

N. saluenensis One of the easier species to grow. This has its leaves usually in pairs, but occasionally threes, and saucer-shaped flowers about 9 cm (3½ in) in diameter. They can be white or pink, spotted near the base of the segments, which are not frilled at the margins.

ORNITHOGALUM

The familiar star of Bethlehem belongs to a very large genus with many species in Europe, western Asia and South Africa, the last of which are not hardy and scarcely known in cultivation except for the chincherinchee, *O. thyrsoides*. They are typically white with a green stripe along the outside of each perianth segment, though some lack this, and a few of the African species have green or yellow flowers. The hardy northern hemisphere species fall into two groups, with either long, narrow racemes of flowers or flat-topped 'heads' with the flowers facing upwards. They are mostly very easy to grow in sunny positions in reasonably well-drained soil. The following are likely to be found in catalogues, but there is much confusion at present over the application of names; modern nomenclature has been avoided until the plants have been identified correctly.

O. arabicum An unusual, early summer-flowering Mediterranean species with several wide basal leaves and 50–75 cm (20–30 in) stems carrying a flat-topped head of large, white flowers with a blackish ovary in the centre, giving a marked black-eyed appearance. It is not very hardy and needs a warm, sunny position against a wall for protection.

O. balansae A dwarf mountain species from Turkey, very suitable for a rock garden. It has two or three shiny green leaves and 5–10 cm (2–4 in) stems carrying up to five upward-facing white flowers with green backs to the segments. Early spring flowering.

O. lanceolatum This species from Turkey and Lebanon produces a tidy rosette of broad green leaves, and in spring a central, near-stemless head of white flowers striped green on the outside. It is one of the more attractive species for a rock garden.

O. narbonense A very common Mediterranean and Asiatic plant flowering in summer. It has long racemes of starry white flowers which are only slightly marked with green on the outside. A warm, sunny, well-drained site suits it best.

O. nutans This European species is rather different from most in having 15–30 cm (6–12 in) spikes of drooping flowers with outward-curving tips. They are silvery-white, with a soft green exterior. It is an attractive plant for naturalizing beneath deciduous shrubs, flowering in late spring.

O. pyrenaicum This is from southern Europe and Britain, where it is known as Bath asparagus. It can grow to a metre (3 ft 3 in) tall, but usually much less, in summer with long racemes of small, greenish-yellow, starry flowers striped darker outside.

Ornithogalum nutans

O. tenuifolium This, and several similar species, is a very common plant of the Mediterranean region. It has narrow, linear leaves and a loose raceme of flowers tending to be flat-topped with the flowers facing upwards, pure white on the inside and green striped on the outside. It and its relatives are easily cultivated and are useful for a sunny rock garden or for planting beneath shrubs.

O. thyrsoides The South African chincherinchee, very long-lasting as a cut flower and often seen in florists' shops with its dense, cone-shaped racemes of many flowers, each one cup-shaped, about 2 cm across in white with no green stripes on the outside; it usually grows to about 30–50 cm (12–20 in) in height. It is not hardy but the bulbs can be purchased in spring and planted in a warm, sunny situation for flowering in summer; they can then be lifted in autumn and stored in a frost-free place.

O. umbellatum The common European star of Bethlehem has narrow green leaves with a conspicuous white stripe along the centre. Its flower stems reach 15–30 cm (6–12 in) and carry in spring a loose raceme of large, glistening white, starry flowers facing upwards and hiding the green backs of the segments. It is useful for naturalizing under deciduous shrubs.

Oxalis

A very large and widespread group of plants, not monocotyledons but many of them tuberous-rooted. Some are invasive weeds and should never be allowed near the garden, but there are a few well-behaved species which are well worth growing in the rock garden. They are dwarf plants with attractive leaves with three or more leaflets, sometimes grey and sometimes zoned with purple-brown. The buds are wrapped like an umbrella, unfurling into flattish flowers, mostly with wide petals giving a nicely rounded shape. The tubers can be bought from bulb firms, or from rock plant nurseries in growth in pots.

O. adenophylla This comes from Chile and Argentina and has a large 'bulb' with a soft, felty covering. It is only 3–5 cm (1¼–2 in) high, with attractive leaves consisting of several grey leaflets and in summer has lovely pale pinkish-purple flowers up to 4 cm (1½ in) across. It needs an open, sunny place in a sharply drained, gritty soil mixture.

O. enneaphylla A relative of *O. adenophylla* from Chile and the Falkland Islands, and an equally attractive plant for the rock garden. The grey leaves are cut into many leaflets, amid which nestle the large pink or white flowers up to 5 cm (2 in) in diameter.

O. laciniata From the southern tip of South America, this species has curious long, scaly rhizomes, almost maggot-like. The whole plant is less than 5 cm (2 in) in height, with the grey leaves consisting of narrow wavy leaflets, just overtopped by steely purple flowers which are conspicuously veined darker and have a dark eye in the centre. It flowers in early summer and likes a cool pocket on the rock garden, or a sunny peat garden, and is also excellent for the alpine house.

O. tetraphylla (*O. deppei*) An easily cultivated species from Mexico, about 10 cm (4 in) tall; the clover-like leaves have a brownish-purple zone and these are overtopped by umbels of pinkish-red flowers in summer. It will grow on the rock garden or front of a border in sun or slight shade.

Pancratium

A small genus in the Amaryllidaceae with white, sweetly scented flowers, mostly tropical and only suitable for glasshouse cultivation, but one Mediterranean species is fairly hardy. The common one, often seen by the shores of the Mediterranean, is *P. maritimum*, but this is a very unsatisfactory garden plant, not hardy and not at all free-flowering even in a glasshouse.

P. illyricum A beautiful plant from Corsica, the large bulbs producing strap-like

Flowering Bulbs for the Garden

Oxalis adenophylla

grey leaves and in summer a leafless stem 30–40 cm (12–16 in) tall carrying an umbel of fragrant white flowers each about 8 cm (3 in) across with a short cup in the centre. When given a sheltered spot against a sunny, south-facing wall this is hardy and can be long-lived, but it is a rare plant and not easy to obtain.

Polianthes

A sizeable genus of Mexican bulbs related to the enormous agaves, but only one species is at all well known and available. This is the tuberose, *P. tuberosa*, which is now only cultivated to a small extent though in centuries gone by it was extremely popular.

P. tuberosa When growing well this can reach 1 m (3 ft 3 in) in height when in flower, with several strap-like, greyish-green basal leaves and a loose spike of deliciously fragrant white flowers consisting of a long curved tube and shorter lobes, all in a thick waxy texture. There is also a double form, 'The Pearl', which is more commonly available but possibly less attractive.

In cultivation the tubers are planted in spring and require a rich soil in a warm, sunny situation. Some old rotted manure dug in deeply before planting is recommended. Until flowering time and through the rest of the summer plenty of water must be given, but in the autumn they should be lifted and dried off to be stored in a frost-free place for the winter months.

Puschkinia

These spring-flowering bulbs are closely related to the squills (scilla) and require similar cultural conditions in the garden. There is possibly only one species, occurring widely in the Middle East on mountains near the melting snow.

P. scilloides (*P. libanotica*) Grows to about 5–10 cm (2–4 in) in height with two basal leaves and a dense raceme of pale blue flowers with a dark stripe along the centre of each segment. Each flower is about 1–1.5 cm (about ½ in) in diameter with the segments joined into a short tube, which distinguishes *Puschkinia* from *Scilla*. There is a white form, 'Alba'. It is a good rock garden plant, flowering in March or April.

Puschkinia scilloides

Ranunculus

Of all the many buttercups it is worth mentioning *R. asiaticus* here as it has tuberous roots, like a bunch of claws, which can be dried off and are usually sold by the bulb nurserymen for planting in spring. The wild forms from the eastern Mediterranean region have large, single flowers in bright red, pink, yellow or white, but these have been developed in cultivation

RHODOHYPOXIS

Rhodohypoxis baurii

for over 300 years to give a much wider range, mostly semi-double or double.

They require a sunny, sheltered position with good drainage and should be planted in early spring about 6–8 cm (2½–3½ in) deep with the claws pointing downwards. The collections usually offered by nurseries are mixed double or semi-double forms which may contain a wide range of colours. They grow to about 30 cm (12 in) tall with several large, upward-facing flowers per stem, often looking like small peonies.

In all but very mild districts they will probably not thrive if left in the ground through the winter and are best replaced each spring or lifted and dried each autumn.

RHODOHYPOXIS

There are few dwarf summer-flowering bulbs, so these bright and unusual little plants from the Drakensberg Mountains of Natal and Lesotho are particularly welcome. They grow to only about 4–8 cm (1½–3 in) in height and flower for an extremely long period, at least from May until August. The best type of soil is sandy and peaty, and they need a sunny position which is slightly protected from severe frosts in winter. If grown in pots in the alpine house they should be almost dried out in winter. The small tubers can be planted in spring before growth begins, or at almost any time during the growing season provided that they are replanted straight away and not allowed to dry out.

R. baurii produces a tuft of linear, hairy leaves among which are produced a long succession of upward-facing flowers which range in colour from white through shades of pink to deep red. Each flower is about 2–3 cm (about 1 in) in diameter and has broad perianth segments which are bent inwards at the base to close the centre of the flower so that no stamens are visible.

There are quite a number of named varieties of *R. baurii*, but most nurseries sell them mixed.

Romulea

A little-known but quite large genus in the Iridaceae, related to crocus with similar but smaller upright, funnel-shaped flowers with only a short perianth tube. There are several species around the Mediterranean, one of which also occurs in Britain, and many in South Africa, though the latter species are all tender and require a frost-free glasshouse. The Mediterranean species are mostly rather small-flowered and of restricted garden value, but one of the most common is worthwhile for growing in a rock garden or alpine house. They require well drained soil in full sun, where they will flower in spring.

R. bulbocodium A dwarf plant with flower stems only about 5 cm (2 in) in height with longer leaves which are very narrow and wiry. The erect flowers open out wide to about 3 cm (1¼ in) across and are bluish-lilac with a yellow throat in the best colour forms. The tiny, colchicum-like corms should be planted in autumn about 5 cm (2 in) deep.

Romulea bulbocodium

Scilla

The squills, best known for their blue spring flowers, are a surprisingly large group of plants distributed widely through Europe and Asia to India and Japan and down through tropical Africa to South Africa, with spring-, summer- and autumn-flowering species. Most of the European and Asiatic ones are hardy and well worth growing, though only a limited number are commercially available. These are mostly blue-flowered, sometimes with white or pink versions. Their bulbs should in most cases be planted in autumn about 5 cm (2 in) deep.

S. autumnalis As its name indicates, this Mediterranean and British species flowers in the autumn, usually early, and has no leaves when the 5–15 cm (2–6 in) racemes of small, starry flowers appear. They vary from pale lilac to blue or purple; though not very showy, it is an interesting little bulb for the sunny rock garden or alpine house. The thread-like leaves appear shortly after the flowers.

S. bifolia A very easily cultivated European and Turkish species, only 5–10 cm (2–4 in) in height, usually with two basal leaves and rather loose racemes of small, deep mauve-blue, starry flowers. It is useful for the rock garden or for naturalizing beneath deciduous shrubs, as it will tolerate partial shade. 'Alba' is a white form, 'Rosea' is pink, and 'Praecox' a particularly robust large-flowered version. *S. bifolia* flowers in February or March.

S. bithynica A slightly later spring squill from Turkey, flowering in March or April, with several strap-like basal leaves and racemes of flattish, bright mid-blue flowers, up to 15 cm (6 in) tall. It is a good plant for naturalizing in dampish, semi-shaded places or a cool spot on the rock garden. *S. messenaica* is almost identical from a garden value point of view.

S. campanulata (*S. hispanica*) The Spanish bluebell, which is sometimes referred to the genus *Endymion* or *Hyacinthoides*. It is a robust bluebell up to 40 cm (16 in) in height with glossy, strap-shaped basal leaves and loose racemes of semi-pendent bell-like flowers in blue, pink or white. It is an excellent late-spring bulb for planting in groups in a sunny or semi-shaded border. Unlike the English bluebell (below) the raceme is not nodding at the apex and the flowers are not held all on one side of the stem.

S. greilhuberi This is sometimes listed as S. hohenackeri, which is similar but botanically distinct and much more rare in cultivation. S. greilhuberi produces long, linear leaves in the autumn, then in March or April 10–15 cm (4–6 in) racemes of lilac-blue flowers, which have reflexed segments when fully open. It is easily cultivated in semi-shade. S. hohenackeri is smaller and produces its tidier leaves in the spring.

S. italica This comes from southern and western Europe, has several narrow basal leaves and 15–20 cm (6–8 in) dense, pyramid-shaped racemes of starry pale to mid-blue flowers. Each flower is accompanied by two longish tapered bracts, which distinguish it from the somewhat similar S. bithynica, which has only one minute bract per flower. S. italica is an attractive spring-flowering squill for the rock garden or sunny border.

S. lilio-hyacinthus An unusual western European species with a curious large, yellowish, scaly bulb like a lily. The broad basal leaves are shiny green in a rosette, out of the centre of which is produced a 15–25 cm (6–10 in) raceme of pale lilac-blue flowers in early summer. It is easily grown in a semi-shaded position in soil that is rich in humus. 'Alba' is an attractive white form.

S. nutans (S. non-scripta, Endymion non-scripta or Hyacinthoides non-scripta) The familiar English bluebell, with its one-sided racemes of tubular blue, pink or white flowers. It is a perfect plant for naturalizing in semi-shade but can become a nuisance in the rock garden and should be avoided in small gardens.

S. peruviana A robust species from southern Europe, with many broad basal leaves which appear in autumn, and large, conical racemes 15–25 cm (6–10 in) tall, and up to 10 cm (4 in) or even more wide at the base. The many flowers are a deep, steely blue, or white in the form 'Alba'. To flower well it needs a hot, sunny situation with the tip of the bulbs level with the surface.

S. pratensis (S. litardieri) A showy species from Yugoslavia, 10–20 cm (4–8 in) in height when in flower in June, with narrow basal leaves and densely flowered, long, cylindrical racemes of small, bright blue flowers. It is easily cultivated in a sunny, well-drained position. S. amethystina is only a form of this species, not a true species of its own.

S. scilloides From China and Japan, an unusual species in that it produces 15–20 cm (6–8 in) racemes of pink flowers between August and October, accompanied by the narrow basal leaves which remain green until the next summer. It is a hardy plant for a sunny position.

S. siberica The much-loved Siberian squill, notable for its few nodding, brilliant blue, bell-like flowers on stems only 5–15 cm (2–6 in) tall. It often flowers in late winter or very early in the spring, opening as the leaves and buds push through the ground and carrying on for several weeks. 'Spring Beauty' is a good deep blue form, and 'Alba' is white-flowered. It is an excellent rock garden plant, and is also very effective naturalized under deciduous shrubs.

S. tubergeniana (S. mischtschenkoana) This dwarf species from Iran is similar to S. siberica in having a few bell-shaped flowers which, in this case, open out almost flat in the sun, but they are pale blue with a darker blue stripe along the centre of each segment. Its flowers open as they emerge from the soil in late winter to early spring, and continue until the stems have reached 10–15 cm (4–6 in). It is an excellent plant for a rock garden or semi-shaded border.

S. verna A small, not very showy species from Europe and British coasts. It has narrow leaves and short dense, almost head-like racemes of lilac-blue flowers in early summer. Suitable for a sunny rock garden.

Sparaxis

These South African cormous plants are known as harlequin flowers as their flattish flowers come in a great array of colours. They are not hardy but can be planted in a sunny position for flowering in summer, the corms being purchased in spring. They must be lifted again before the autumn frosts.

Sparaxis grow to about 15 cm (6 in) tall with fans of small, iris-like leaves and spikes of flat flowers each up to 5 cm (2 in) across. In the mixed collections that are usually offered there will probably be orange, red, pinkish or white forms, usually with zones of purple and yellow in the centre.

Sternbergia lutea

Sternbergia

A small genus in the amaryllis family from southern Europe and western Asia whose species are notable for their yellow crocus-shaped flowers in autumn, though two rare species have their flowers in spring, *S. fischeriana*, which is yellow, and *S. candida*, which has white flowers. The most common, *S. lutea*, is the best garden plant. They all require planting in hot, sunny situations in well-drained soil and are particularly good on alkaline soils; the bulbs are obtained in early autumn and planted about 7 cm (about 3 in) deep. They are sometimes offered nowadays as 'autumn daffodils', though there is very little resemblance.

S. clusiana The largest-flowered species, from Turkey and Iran. The large, greeny-yellow goblets about 10 cm (4 in) tall appear before the leaves in autumn, followed by greyish, strap-shaped leaves in winter and spring. It is better in a bulb frame than in the open garden.

S. lutea In a sunny place by a south wall this Mediterranean species is one of the best autumn bulbs, with large, deep yellow goblets amid deep green leaves, the whole plant about 15 cm (6 in) tall at flowering time in September or October.

S. sicula This is like a smaller, more compact version of *S. lutea*, an excellent plant but less easy to obtain.

Tecophilaea

A choice South American bulb from the Andes, known as the Chilean blue crocus. There is one superb species, thought to be extinct in the wild but which can still be obtained from specialist bulb nurseries. It is hardy and will grow outdoors in a well-drained, sunny situation, but it is expensive and few people entrust it to the open garden, preferring to cosset it in an alpine house or bulb frame. The bulbs are planted in autumn and flower in spring and should then be dried out for the summer, but not sun-baked.

T. cyanocrocus Crocus-like corms produce one or two narrow leaves and flower stems to about 5–10 cm (2–4 in) carrying one funnel-shaped flower which opens wide to about 3 cm ($1\frac{1}{4}$ in) across. The colour is normally an intense deep blue, but 'Leichtlinii' is paler blue with a large white eye, and 'Violacea' has purplish flowers.

TIGRIDIA

A most interesting genus in the Iridaceae, with iris-shaped flowers that unfortunately last only a few hours. However, a succession is produced over two or three weeks, and one of the species is so colourful as to be an excellent addition to the garden for a summer display. The bulbs should be planted in spring when the frosts are over, about 8–10 cm ($3\frac{1}{2}$–4 in) deep in a warm, sunny situation in well-drained, preferably sandy soil. They require plenty of water in summer, at least until they have flowered in July and August.

T. pavonia The tiger flower has pleated, sword-shaped leaves and grows to about 45 cm (18 in) tall. The upward-facing flowers are produced in long succession and open in the early morning; they are up to 15 cm (6 in) across with three large outer segments, and three small inner ones forming a bowl-shaped centre which is either heavily blotched red or plain. The main colour may be orange-red, yellow or white, with or without a blotched centre. It is usual to be offered mixed collections, though there are named varieties. The bulbs must generally be lifted in winter and stored away from frost, though in mild areas they can be left in the ground permanently.

Tigridia pavonia

Trillium grandiflorum

Trillium

These lovely, mainly North American, tuberous-rooted relatives of the lily family should not be dried out like most bulbs, so they are usually sold as growing plants in pots; if they are sent out by a bulb nursery in the dormant state they should have damp peat or moss wrapped around them. Planting can take place during any reasonably mild period from autumn through to early spring, or with pot-grown plants at any time. They are best given a semi-shaded site which does not dry out too much, with a good humus content in the soil. The larger species are planted not less than 10 cm (4 in) deep, the smaller ones such as *T. rivale* only 3–4 cm (a good 1½ in). A peat garden suits them admirably.

Trilliums are so called because their leaves and flower parts are in threes. Only a few are generally available, but several others can be found by hunting in the specialist catalogues. They all flower in April or May.

T. erectum From eastern North America, this species has stems about 30 cm (12 in) tall, with a whorl of three broad leaves overtopped by a stalked, flattish flower about 3–4 cm (1½ in) in diameter, usually in deep claret-red though there is a white form ('Album'), and a less attractive greenish-yellow.

T. grandiflorum Probably the finest species, the wake robin of the eastern United States. It grows to about 30 cm (12 in) with a whorl of broad, plain green leaves and a huge erect flower with three white petals giving a spread of about 7–10 cm (3–4 in). *T. ovatum* from the western States is very similar but slightly smaller.

T. rivale A delightful little species from Oregon and California, only 5 cm (2 in) or so in height, with three-petalled flowers about 3 cm (1¼ in) across, in white spotted with red. It is ideal for a cool, raised pocket on the rock garden or peat garden.

T. sessile of gardens (probably *T. cuneatum*) A lovely North American species forming clumps to about 20 cm (8 in) tall, with broad leaves beautifully mottled light and dark green. The flowers are sessile on the leaves, facing upwards and rather shuttlecock-shaped, with three narrow, deep plum-coloured petals. Var. *luteum* has yellowish-green flowers.

Triteleia see Brodiaea

Tulipa

The tulips need no introduction for their bright spring flowers are known to all but, apart from the very familiar hybrid groups such as Cottage, Darwin, Lily-flowered, Parrots and Rembrandts, there are the wild species, many of which are equally lovely garden plants. Some are so dwarf as to be excellent for the rock garden, while others have a delicacy of form lost in the very large garden hybrids.

Nearly all tulips, whether bedding types or wild species, need sunny situations with good drainage, and will not do so well if

Trillium sessile

their bulbs lie shaded and damp during their dormant period in summer. In many gardens it will be found that they are best dug up and dried once the foliage has turned yellow; in this way they can be kept for year after year in good condition. Given the right conditions, however, clumps of tulips planted informally around the garden thrive for many years and provide welcome splashes of colour in the mid to late spring after many of the earlier bulbs have finished their display.

Tulips are planted in autumn, in fact they can be left later than most bulbs – as late as October or November is possible if the weather is reasonable. They prefer deep planting, the smaller species about 10 cm (4 in) deep and the large hybrid bulbs up to 25 cm (10 in) deep on sandy soils. On heavy soils it is best to improve drainage by working in some sharp sand.

Apart from the wild species described below there are the hybrids, which have been classified according to various characteristics; a selection of these is given, in their groups, after the species. Specialist bulb nurseries will from time to time certainly have other species available, and there are also a great many other hybrids.

T. acuminata Not a wild species but a curious cultivar, 45–60 cm (18–24 in) tall with long, pointed segments in red and yellow.

T. aucheriana Comes from Iran and is only 8–10 cm (3½–4 in), with lilac-pink flowers with a yellow centre.

T. batalinii A Central Asiatic species with narrow, wavy grey leaves and pale yellow flowers on 10 cm (4 in) stems. There are forms of this with an orange suffusion on the outside, such as 'Bronze Charm'.

T. clusiana The lady tulip from Iran to Kashmir has slender white flowers flushed crimson on the outside on stems to about 30 cm (12 in). *T. chrysantha* is sometimes listed as a variety of this, with similar flowers in yellow stained with red outside.

T. stellata is also related to *T. clusiana*, but has white flowers with a yellow centre, again stained red outside.

T. eichleri A dramatic Central Asiatic species, with 25–30 cm (10–12 in) stems carrying enormous, striking reddish-orange black-centred flowers 10–12 cm (4–5 in) across.

T. fosteriana A Central Asiatic species, 25–40 cm (10–16 in) in height, which has broad grey leaves and large, bright red flowers with a black blotch in the centre and often with a paler gold, buff or fawn 'wash' on the outside. In addition to the wild species there are some cultivars including 'Madame Lefeber' (brilliant red), 'Purissima' (white) and 'Orange Emperor' (orange). A hybrid group, between *T. fosteriana* and the Darwin tulips, is given below under the heading Darwin hybrids (see page 42).

T. greigii A wonderful Central Asiatic tulip which is sturdy and only 20–25 cm (8–10 cm) in height, with broad leaves that are beautifully streaked and blotched with purple. In the wild species the flowers are deep red with a black blotch in the centre, but there is now a great range of cultivars and hybrids known as the Greigii tulips such as 'Red Riding Hood' (bright red), 'Corsage' (orange, red and apricot mixture), 'Plaisir' (red, margined with yellow), 'Toronto' (two or three flowers per stem, rosy coloured, tinged red).

There are also hybrids with *T. kauffmanniana* (see below).

T. hageri This comes from Greece and Turkey and has brownish-orange flowers with a hint of yellow and green with a dark, almost blackish centre. It is about 25–30 cm (10–12 in) tall. *T. orphanidea* and *T. whittallii* are similar, and probably only forms of it.

T. humilis A dwarf Turkish and Iranian species only 7–15 cm (3–6 in) tall, with narrow, greyish leaves in a rosette on the ground and magenta-pink flowers with a yellow centre. There are many variations, sometimes called *T. violacea* and *T. pulchella*, with flowers in the purple and violet shades. 'Violet Queen' is a good cultivar currently offered in catalogues.

T. kaufmanniana The waterlily tulip from Central Asia is, in its wild form, a dwarf plant only 10–20 cm (4–8 in) tall, with broad grey leaves and creamy flowers flushed red on the outside. There are, however, many variants and hybrids, notably with *T. greigii*, which has imparted its lovely purple-striped leaves. The hybrids range from about 12–25 cm (5–10 in) in height and include 'Stresa' (yellow with a crimson stain outside), 'Shakespeare' (orange and pinkish suffusion, yellowish inside), 'Gluck' (pale yellow flecked brown inside, red edged yellow outside), 'Berlioz' (yellow).

T. kolpakowskiana A slender species with narrow grey leaves from Soviet Central Asia, about 15–20 cm (6–8 in) tall with smallish, narrow-petalled flowers in yellow with a red exterior.

T. linifolia A Central Asiatic species related to *T. batalinii* and with similar narrow, grey, undulating leaves. The flowers, carried on stems 10–15 cm (4–6 in) tall, are, however, bright red. *T. maximowiczii* is very similar.

T. marjolettii Grows to about 35–45 cm (14–18 in) in height, with broad grey leaves and a soft primrose-yellow flower faintly suffused with red on the exterior. It is from southern France.

T. praestans This is another of the big, red-flowered Central Asiatic species, but this particular one produces up to four flowers per stem and they have no blackish blotch in the centre. It grows to about 30 cm (12 in) tall.

T. saxatilis An unusual species from Crete, which has glossy green leaves and pinkish-lilac, yellow-centred flowers on stems 30–40 cm (12–16 in) tall. It spreads by stolons to form patches, but is not very free-flowering and in order to do well must be given a very hot, sunny situation.

T. sprengeri The latest tulip, often not opening its flowers until late May or early June. It is a Turkish species, about

Tulipa aucheriana

Tulipa hageri

30–35 cm (12–14 in) tall, with glossy green leaves and scarlet-red flowers with a paler, almost gold, exterior. It is very easy and seeds itself freely, but is still a little expensive.

T. sylvestris A slender species from European woodlands, including Britain, growing to about 30 cm (12 in) with pendent buds opening to yellow flowers tinged with green on the exterior. It is easy to grow and will naturalize under deciduous shrubs, but it does not flower very freely.

T. tarda One of the best of the dwarf species, only about 10 cm (4 in) in height with a rosette of narrow, greyish leaves and up to five flowers per stem, white with a large yellow zone in the centre. It is a native of Soviet Central Asia.

T. turkestanica From Central Asia, this species grows to about 20 cm (8 in) tall, with narrow grey leaves and several smallish white flowers with yellow centres and a greenish tinge on the exterior. *T. biflora* is very similar, with only one or two flowers per stem.

T. urumiensis This is a dwarf species from northern Iran, only 10–15 cm (4–6 in) tall with a rosette of narrow, greyish leaves and relatively large yellow flowers with a bronzy-green exterior.

Hybrids There are fifteen recognized groups of tulips, but I have included only the horticulturally more important ones, with a selection of cultivars in each case.

EARLY SINGLE
Early to mid April, mostly 40 cm (16 in) or less tall and with rather rounded flowers. Varieties include 'Bellona' (golden yellow), 'De Wet' (orange), 'Keizerskroon' (bright red, edged yellow), 'Princess Irene' (orange with flame-shaped purple marks outside).

EARLY DOUBLE
Early to mid April, mostly 30 cm (12 in) or

less in height. Tightly double or semi-double flowers. Varieties include 'Orange Nassau' (deep red), 'Vermeer' (red with petals edged yellow), 'Mr van der Hoef' (golden yellow), 'Snow Queen' (white with a yellowish stain inside).

MID SEASON TULIPS
These come slightly later, in mid–late April, and are usually 40–50 cm (16–20 in) tall. They include the Triumph and Mendel tulips. Varieties include 'High Society' (reddish orange fading to orange yellow at the edges), 'Golden Melody' (deep golden yellow), 'Attila' (purplish-violet with whitish centre), 'Lady Diana' (rose red), 'White Dream' (pure white).

MAY FLOWERING TULIPS
These are among the most popular of tulips for bedding out. They are very robust, 60–85 cm (2 ft–2 ft 10 in) tall with large, rounded flowers which come in early May. The Darwin and Cottage tulips are grouped here. There are a great many varieties; recommended ones include 'Queen of Bartigons' (lovely shade of pink), 'La Tulipe Noire' (velvety blackish-purple), 'Halcro' (bright red with orange-red edges), 'Palestrina' (salmon and rose mixture), 'Clara Butt' (soft pink), Niphetos' (creamy yellow).

DARWIN HYBRID TULIPS
These are Darwin tulips crossed with the Central Asiatic red-flowered species *T. fosteriana*. They are about 60 cm (24 in) tall, flower in late April and have large oval buds and very grey foliage. Varieties include 'Golden Apeldoorn' (yellow, flecked red), 'Hollands Glory' (orange red), 'Jewel of Spring' (pale yellow with red margins and a black centre).

LILY-FLOWERED TULIPS
Very distinctive varieties with long, pointed petals arching outwards at the tips. They flower in May and are about 45–60 cm (18–24 in) in height. Good varieties are 'Westpoint' (yellow), 'White Triumphator' (pure white), 'Maytime' (purple edged with white), 'Elegant Lady' (cream, edged rose), 'Queen of Sheba' (red, edged yellow).

VIRIDIFLORA TULIPS
For those who like the unusual, these have green markings on the exterior. They flower in late May and are usually 30–40 cm (12–16 in) tall. Varieties include 'Artist' (rose pink with a broad green band outside), 'Hummingbird' (yellow with a broad green stain outside), 'Greenland' (rich cyclamen pink with a green triangular mark outside).

REMBRANDT TULIPS
These have splashes and streaks of brilliant colours on a differently coloured ground. They flower in May and are about 60 cm (24 in) tall. Varieties include 'Sorbet' (near-white with red flame-like marks), 'Insulinde' (a cream ground with various purple and bronze markings), 'San Marino' (yellow with red, flame-like marks).

PAEONY-FLOWERED LATE DOUBLE TULIPS
These are double varieties that flower later than the 'Early Double' group, in late April or early May. They are about 45–55 cm (18–22 in) in height. Varieties include 'Mount Tacoma' (white), 'Gold Medal' (golden yellow), 'Lilac Perfection' (lilac shading to white at the centre), 'May Wonder' (rose pink with green splashes on the outside).

PARROT TULIPS AND FRINGED TULIPS
These have huge flowers with the petals fringed with hair-like processes, or lacerated along the edges. They can be up to 20 cm (8 in) across on stems 45–60 cm (18–24 in) tall and are produced in mid May. Varieties include 'Black Parrot' (blackish maroon, lacerated at the edges), 'Burgundy Lace' (carmine red with a crystalline fringe on the edges), 'Fantasy' (pink with green splashes and lacerated edges), 'Gay Presto' or 'Estelle Rijnveld' (lacerated petals, white with bright red splashes and flame-like marks).

WATSONIA

A large South African genus barely known in cultivation, and resembling gladiolus in their spikes of funnel-shaped flowers, though these are more regular in shape than those of gladiolus. They are mostly large plants, capable of making clumps of corms and tufts of leathery, sword-shaped leaves from which arise the wiry flower stems in summer. Only a few species are in cultivation, and these are uncommon. Watsonias need to be planted in a sheltered sunny position with the large corms at least 10 cm (4 in) deep. If they can be obtained in spring, this is the safest time to plant them; a south-facing wall provides the right sort of protection.

W. pyramidata (*W. rosea*) A robust species up to 1.5 m (5 ft) or more when in flower. It has pink or mauve, widely funnel-shaped flowers in late summer.

W. versveldii Branched flower stems with pink flowers stained red in the throat.

W. wordsworthiana Tubular flowers of a deep purple colour, and similar in shape are those of *W. fourcadei* but in a paler, reddish-purple.

ZANTEDESCHIA

Only one species in this South African genus can be cultivated out in the open garden, the well-known arum lily, *Z. aethiopica*, which has large, white, upward-facing trumpets with an orange, pencil-like spadix in the centre, carried on stout stems to 60 cm (24 in) in height. The leaves are broadly arrow-shaped and would be evergreen were it not for the frosts in winter. However, loss of these leaves in winter does not seem to damage the plant and some new ones are produced in spring as soon as the weather warms up.

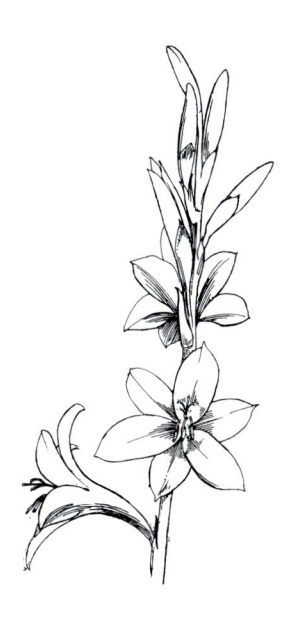

The best situation for the arum lily is at the edge of a pool, in moist soil with its tubers planted 15 cm (6 in) or more deep. It will also grow satisfactorily if they are planted well below water level where they cannot be frosted. It is said that the cultivar 'Crowborough' is the hardiest form.

ZEPHYRANTHES

Unfortunately nearly all of the many lovely species in this large genus of American Amaryllidaceae are tender, and only one species, *Z. candida*, can be described as reliably hardy. This has large, crocus-shaped white flowers in September or October, facing upwards on 10–15 cm (4–6 in) stalks amid the rush-like green leaves. It is best cultivated in a sunny border at the foot of a south-facing wall, along with other bulbs with similar requirements such as *Amaryllis* and *Nerine bowdenii*.

ZIGADENUS

A mainly North American group of bulbs with racemes of starry, greenish flowers in summer, not very showy but interesting for the bulb specialist and not unattractive when grown in a group. They are easy to grow in the open border in a sunny or semi-shaded situation.

Z. elegans Grows to about 60–70 cm (24–28 in) with strap-shaped, greyish green leaves. The flowers, carried in a large, loose raceme, are pale green with a darker, glistening nectary near the base of each segment. *Z. glaucus* and *Z. fremontii* are very similar.

Watsonia pyramidata

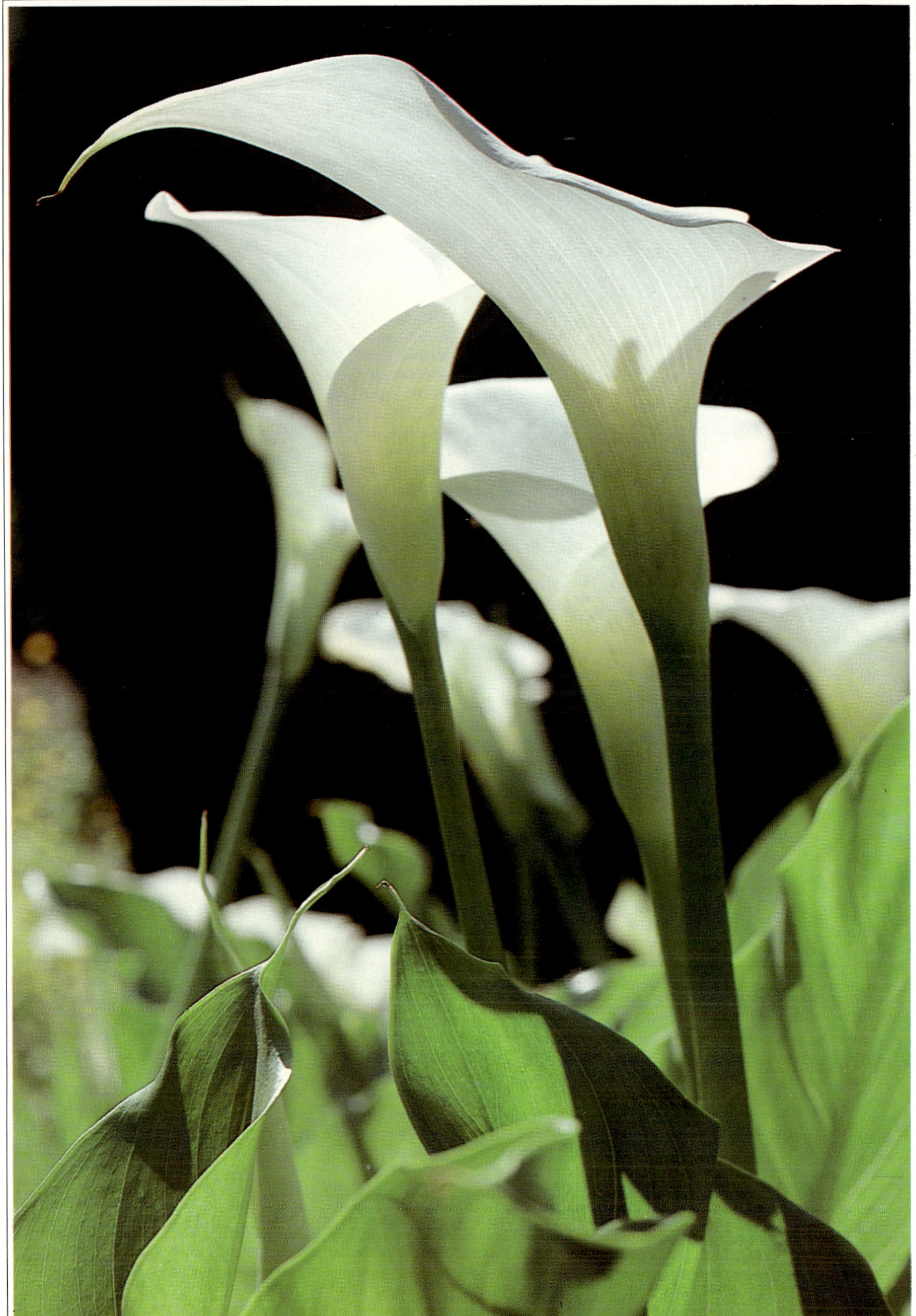

Bulbs for Selected Sites

Bulbs for herbaceous borders

(Those that need to be lifted for the winter are marked w)
Acidanthera bicolor (*Gladiolus callianthus*) (w)
Allium aflatunense
A. christophii (*A. albopilosum*)
A. karataviense
A. pulchellum
A. rosenbachianum
A. sphaerocephalon
Anemone coronaria
A. pavonina
Arisaema candidissimum
Camassia – any species
Crinum powellii
Crocosmia – any species or hybrids
Crocus vernus (large Dutch cultivars)
Curtonus paniculatus
Dierama pulcherrimum
Dracunculus vulgaris
Eucomis bicolor
Fritillaria imperialis cultivars
F. persica
Galtonia candicans (w)
Gladiolus byzantinus
G. callianthus (w)
Gladiolus hybrids (w)
Hyacinthus orientalis cultivars
Iris bucharica
I. magnifica
I. latifolia (*I. xphioides*) cultivars
I. xiphium cultivars
Dutch iris cultivars
Leucojum aestivum
Lilium amabile
L. auratum
L. cernuum
L. concolor
L. croceum
L. dauricum
L. davidii and var. *willmottiae*
L. henryi
L. pumilum
L. pyrenaicum
L. regale
L. speciosum
L. tigrinum
Trumpet hybrids
Asiatic hybrids
Moraea spathulata
Narcissus cyclamineus hybrids
N. triandrus hybrids
Any other tall hybrid daffodil and narcissus
Ornithogalum thyrsoides (w)
Tigridia pavonia cultivars (w)
Tulipa fosteriana and its hybrids
T. greigii hybrids
T. hageri
T. kaufmanniana hybrids
Any of the large-flowered hybrids
Zantedeschia aethiopica

Opposite: *Zantedeschia aethiopica*

Left: *Allium karataviense*, a superb border plant

Bulbs for Growing in Grass

Camassia quamash (*C. esculenta*)
Colchicum autumnale
C. byzantinum
C. speciosum
Crocus flavus ('Dutch Yellow')
C. nudiflorus
C. speciosus
C. tommasinianus
C. vernus (large Dutch cultivars)
Erythronium dens-canis
Fritillaria meleagris
Galanthus nivalis
Iris reticulata
I. histrioides
Leucojum aestivum
L. vernum
Muscari neglectum (*M. racemosum*)
Narcissus bulbocodium
N. cyclamineus and hybrids
N. triandrus
Any of the large garden hybrids
Nectaroscordum (*Allium*) *dioscoridis*
Ornithogalum nutans
O. umbellatum
Scilla bifolia
S. campanulata (*S. hispanica*)
S. nutans (*S. non-scripta*)
S. siberica

Bulbs for Semi-Shade in Shrub Borders and Under Trees

Allium moly
Anemone apennina
A. blanda
A. nemorosa
A. ranunculoides
Arisaema – all species
Arum italicum 'Pictum'
Brimeura amethystina (*Hyacinthus amethystinus*)
Camassia – all species
Chionodoxa – all species
Corydalis bulbosa
C. solida
Crocus banaticus
Cyclamen coum
C. hederifolium
Eranthis hyemalis
Erythronium – all species
Fritillaria camschatcensis
F. pontica
Galanthus – all species and varieties
Ipheion uniflorum
Leucojum aestivum
L. vernum
Lilium amabile
L. auratum
L. hansonii
L. mackliniae
L. martagon
L. pardalinum
L. regale
L. speciosum
L. superbum
L. tigrinum
Trumpet hybrids
Bellingham hybrids
Muscari neglectum
Narcissus cyclamineus and hybrids
Nectaroscordum (*Allium*) *dioscoridis*
Nomocharis – all species
Ornithogalum nutans
O. umbellatum
Scilla bifolia
S. bithynica
S. campanulata (*S. hispanica*)
S. lilio-hyacinthus
S. nutans (*S. non-scripta*)
S. siberica
S. tubergeniana
Trillium – all species

Bulbs for rock gardens and raised beds

Allium flavum
A. oreophilum
Anemone blanda
A. nemorosa cultivars
A. ranunculoides (shady spot)
Brimeura amethystina (*Hyacinthus amethystinus*)
Chionodoxa – any species
Colchicum agrippinum
Corydalis solida
Crocus – almost any mentioned in text
Cyclamen – any hardy species
Eranthis hyemalis
Erythronium – all species (for shady spot)
Fritillaria meleagris
F. pontica
F. pyrenaica
Galanthus – any species and cultivars (semi-shade)
Ipheion uniflorum
Iris danfordiae
I. histrioides
I. reticulata and varieties
I. winogradowii
Leucojum autumnale
L. vernum
Lilium martagon
L. pumilum (*L. tenuifolium*)
Muscari azureum
M. botryoides
Narcissus asturiensis
N. bulbocodium
N. cyclamineus
N. triandrus
Ornithogalum balansae
Oxalis adenophylla
O. enneaphylla
Puschkinia scilloides
Rhodohypoxis baurii
Scilla bifolia
S. siberica
S. tubergeniana
Trillium grandiflorum
T. sessile
Tulipa batalinii
T. clusiana
T. greigii
T. humilis
T. kaufmanniana
T. linifolia
T. sprengeri
T. tarda
T. turkestanica
T. urumiensis

Iris histrioides

Cyclamen coum, an ideal plant to brighten up the cold greenhouse or bulb frame in winter

Bulbs for unheated frames and greenhouses

Bulbocodium vernum
Colchicum luteum
Corydalis diphylla
C. solida
Crocus ancyrensis
C. angustifolius
C. biflorus
C. chrysanthus
C. corsicus
C. fleischeri
C. goulimyi
C. hadriaticus
C. imperati
C. korolkowii
C. laevigatus
C. minimus
C. niveus
C. tournefortii
Cyclamen – any species
Fritillaria – any species except *F. imperialis* and *F. persica*
Iris – any of the Reticulata group and Juno group
Leucojum autumnale
L. nicaeense
L. roseum

Merendera montana
Muscari azureum
M. macrocarpum
M. moschatum (muscarimi)
Narcissus asturiensis
N. bulbocodium
N. cantabricus
N. triandrus
Ornithogalum balansae
Oxalis adenophylla
O. enneaphylla
Puschkinia scilloides
Rhodohypoxis baurii
Romulea bulbocodium
Scilla scilloides
S. siberica
S. tubergeniana
Sternbergia sicula
S. fischeriana
Tecophilaea cyanocrocus
Tulipa aucheriana
T. batalinii
T. humilis
T. tarda
T. urumiensis

Glossary

acid Soil that has a pH of less than 7; opposite of alkaline; often peaty.

acute Pointed.

alkaline Soil that has a pH of more than 7; opposite of acid; chalk or limestone soils.

alternate Leaves that are alternating up the stem, not opposite or in a whorl.

axil Junction between leaf and stem.

basal Applied to leaves that arise directly from the bulb or rootstock, rather than being carried on the stem.

basal core, basal plate The central core of tissue of a bulb to which the fleshy scales are attached.

bract A modified leaf that is adjacent to the stalk of a flower or the flower itself.

bulb A storage organ that usually consists of several fleshy scales (sometimes only one or two) attached to a basal plate of solid tissue.

bulbil Small bulbs produced on the stem or in the leaf axils, or in the inflorescence.

bulblet Small bulbs produced around the parent bulb.

channelled Leaves that have a v-shaped cross-section.

compost A mixture of ingredients used for potting, sometimes referred to as a potting medium. The word compost is also used to describe rotted organic material.

corm A storage organ consisting of solid tissue, not scaly like a bulb; it is completely replaced each year.

corolla Usually used in connection with narcissus in the bulb world, it refers to the six perianth segments, as opposed to the corona which is the cup or trumpet.

cultivar A variant of any species or hybrid which is considered distinct from a horticultural point of view.

dormant A stage in a plant's life cycle when no active growth is visible, though in the case of a bulb buds may be forming inside.

epiphytic A plant that grows up in the air with no contact with the soil, such as on the branches of a tree; it is not, however, parasitic.

fall Used to describe iris flowers; the three, usually larger, outer perianth segments ('petals') which have a reflexed blade, hence 'falling' outwards.

frame lights Glass or plastic structures to cover frames for protection from the cold or wet.

glaucous Leaves that are covered with a greyish, waxy coat, as with cabbage leaves.

half hardy Bulbs that can be planted out in spring for the summer months and lifted again for the winter.

humus Well rotted vegetable matter such as leafmould, horse manure, peat, etc.

hybrid A cross between two plants, usually of different species but not necessarily – it may be between forms, varieties, subspecies, etc.

keeled Leaves that have a strong rib beneath, forming a distinct ridge.

lanceolate Tapered towards each end, with the broadest point below the middle.

linear Rather narrow, with the margins more or less parallel.

monocotyledon Plants that have a single seed leaf or cotyledon, not a pair.

opposite Leaves that arise as a pair, one on each side of a stem.

pedicel The stem of a single flower.

peduncle The stem common to several flowers, each of which is in turn carried on a pedicel.

perianth In the monocotyledons this refers to the six showy 'petals' or perianth segments of the flower, usually in two whorls of three, an inner and an outer whorl.

perianth tube In some flowers the six segments are united at the base into a tube, known as the perianth tube.

propagation The act of increasing the numbers of a plant by seed, cuttings, bulb division, etc.

raceme A type of flower arrangement, as in the bluebell, where there is an elongated central axis with flowers carried separately along its length, each on its own pedicel or stalk.

reflexed The tips of petals or perianth segments that bend back, as in a cyclamen flower or erythronium.

rhizome A storage organ that is really a modified stem and capable of producing shoots and roots. It normally progresses horizontally and may be below ground or level with the surface (as in many irises).

rosette A cluster of leaves densely packed together in a wheel-like form, often flat on the ground but sometimes partially upright.

scales The separate fleshy 'leaves' which go to make up a bulb.

spadix The thick, fleshy, pencil-like organ of an arum 'flower' which carries many very small male and female flowers near the base.

spathe A modified, usually papery leaf which encloses the whole flower cluster in the bud stage; in arums it is the most conspicuous part of the 'flower'.

spike A raceme (see above) in which the individual flowers have no stalks; it is thus usually very dense, as in some grape hyacinths.

spur A hollow tubular or sac-like extension to a petal, often containing nectar, as in corydalis and many orchids.

stamen The male portion of the flower, which produces pollen and consists of the filament (stalk) and anther (pollen-bearing part).

standard In iris flowers, the three inner perianth segments ('petals') which stand erect.

stigma The tip of the female part of the flower which receives the pollen from the anthers as a prelude to fertilization; it may be stalkless or carried on a stalk, the style.

strap-like A leaf or petal that is parallel-sided like a belt or strap, rather wider than linear.

stolon An underground, slender growth produced by a bulb, which gives rise to a small bulb at its tip; a bulb with this potential is said to be stoloniferous.

tessellated With rather squared markings as in Roman mosaic pavements; it can be seen in some fritillaria and colchicum flowers.

top-dressing An extra layer of soil, compost, leafmould, grit, sand, etc., which is placed over bulbs during their dormant period, often for nourishment but sometimes for protection.

trumpet Used to describe daffodils and other narcissus where the corona (see above) is well-developed and roughly trumpet-shaped.

tuber A swollen underground organ that is solid, unlike a bulb which is scaly.

tunic The papery or fibrous coats covering bulbs and corms.

turkscap A type of lily flower in which the perianth segments ('petals') roll back in a turban-like manner.

umbel A type of flower cluster in which the flowers all arise from the same point at the apex of a stem, as in allium species (onions, etc).

variety One of the units of classification below that of species and subspecies; often used loosely in gardening circles instead of cultivar.

whorl Leaves that arise all from the same point on a stem in a circle around it, as in the case of the martagon lily.

Acknowledgements

Line artwork by Howard Ryan

Photographs

Pat Brindley, pages 23, 34, 51, 62, 66, 67, 70, 71 (bottom), 79 (top), 82 (top), 94 (bottom), 102 (bottom), 103, 106, 107, 115, 118. Linda Burgess, pages 50, 58–9. Crown copyright © reproduced with the permission of the controller, Her Majesty's Stationary Office, and the Director, Royal Botanic Gardens, Kew, pages 10, 14, 29, 52. William Davidson/The Hamlyn Publishing Group Limited, pages 91, 102 (top). John Glover, pages 75 (top), 114. Jerry Harpur, pages 6, 26, 30, 39 (Barnsley House, Cirencester), 42 (Yeomans, Oxon), 46 (Chris Grey-Wilson), 99 (bottom). Brian Mathew, pages 19, 22, 35, 43, 54, 55, 63, 71 (top), 74, 75 (bottom), 78, 79 (bottom), 82 (bottom), 83, 86, 94 (top), 99 (top), 110, 111. S. & O. Mathews, pages 38, 95, 98. Photos Horticultural, page 90.

The pictures on pages 16, 20 and 117 are reproduced with the permission of The Royal Botanic Gardens, Kew.

Bibliography

General works on bulbs and their cultivation

Mathew, Brian *Dwarf Bulbs* (Batsford, 1973)
Mathew, Brian *Larger Bulbs* (Batsford, 1978)
Mathew, Brian *The Year Round Bulb Garden* (Souvenir Press, 1986)
Rix, Martyn *Growing Bulbs* (Croom Helm, 1985)
Rix, Martyn and Phillips, Roger *The Bulb Book* (Pan Books, 1981)
Schauenberg, P. *The Bulb Book* (Frederick Warne, 1965)
Synge, P.M. *Collins Guide to Bulbs* (Collins, 1961)

Field guides to bulbs in the wild

Grey-Wilson, C. and Mathew, Brian *Bulbs, the Bulbous Plants of Europe* (Collins, 1981)
Mathew, Brian and Baytop, Turham *The Bulbous Plants of Turkey* (Batsford, 1984)
Wendelbo, Per *Tulips and Irises of Iran* (Tehran, 1977)

Works on individual groups of bulbs

Beck, C. *Fritillaries* (Faber, 1953)
Bowles, E.A. *A Handbook of Crocus and Colchicum* (Hopkinson, 1924; new ed. Bodley Head, 1952; reprinted Waterstone, 1985)
Bowles, E.A. *A Handbook of Narcissus* (Hopkinson, 1934; reprinted Waterstone, 1985)
Hall, A.D. *The Genus Tulipa* (Royal Horticultural Society, 1940)
Jefferson-Brown, M.J. *The Daffodil* (Faber & Faber, 1951)
Mathew, Brian *The Crocus* (Batsford, 1982)
Mathew, Brian *The Iris* (Batsford, 1981)
Stern, F.C. *Snowdrops and Snowflakes* (Royal Horticultural Society, 1956)
Synge, P.M. *Lilies* (Batsford, 1980)

Well illustrated works

Rix, Martyn and Phillips, Roger *The Bulb Book* (Pan Books, 1981)

Curtis's *Botanical Magazine* (now *The Kew Magazine*). This publication still maintains its long tradition of fine colour printing and articles on plants, plant collecting and conservation. Since it was established in 1787 nearly 10,500 colour plates have appeared by many of the best British botanical artists.

Index

Page numbers in italics indicate illustrations d = line drawing

Acidanthera 43, 44, 45
   bicolor 38, *79*, 80
alpine house 28
Allium:
   aflatunense 37, *46*, 60
   caeruleum 60
   callimischon 60
   carinatum 60
   christophii (A. albopilosum) 60
   flavum 60
   giganteum 60
   karataviense 60, 115
   moly 60, *61*
   neapolitanum 60
   oreophilum (A. ostrowskianum) 60
   rosenbachianum 60
   roseum 61
   sphaerocephalon 61
   triquetrum 61
   ursinum 61
Amaryllis belladonna 21, 24, 61
Anemone 57
   apennina 61
   blanda 61
   coronaria 62
      'De Caen' 38
      'St Brigid' 38
   fulgens 62
   nemorosa 62
      'Allenii' *62*
   pavoniana 62
   ranunculoides 62
Anomatheca laxa 62–3
aphids 51
Arisaema:
   candidissimum 63
   consanguineum 63
Arisarum proboscideum 63
Arum:
   creticum 63, *63*
   italicum 63

Baker, J.G. 16
beds:
   in frame and greenhouse 56–7
   raised 28, 40–1, 40d, 117
belladonna lily, see Amaryllis belladonna
benomyl 51
Boissier, Edmund 16, *16*
bonemeal 35
borders:
   herbaceous: bulbs in 36–8, 115
   shrub: bulbs in 34–6, 116
botrytis 50–1
Brimeura 63
   amethystina 64
Brodiaea:
   ixioides 64
   lactea 64
   laxa 64
bulblets: encouraging 47–9, 48d

Bulbocodium vernum 64
bulbs 24d
   growth cycle 21, 25
   meaning and use of term 13
   in wild 21–5
buttercup 32–3

Calochortus:
   albus 54, 64
   barbatus 25, 64
   luteus 64
   uniflorus 64
Camassia 36, 64
   leichtlinii *34*, 65
   quamash (C. esculenta) 65, *66*
Cardiocrinum giganteum 65, *65*
caterpillars 50
Chilean crocus, see Tecophilaea
Chionodoxa 35
   forbesii 65
   luciliae 65
   sardensis 65
climate 21–5
Colchicum 21, 65
   × agrippinum 66
   autumnale 66
   bivonae 66
   byzantinum 66
   cilicium 66
   hybrids 66–7
   luteum 66
   speciosum 66, *66*
collecting: dangers of 17–19
collectors 15–17
compost 41, 42, 54, 56–7
conservation 17–19
container-grown bulbs 28
containers: bulbs in 42–5, *42*, 44d
corm 13, 24d
Corydalis:
   bulbosa (C. cava) 67
   cashmeriana 67
   diphylla 67
   solida 67, *67*
Cotinus coggygria 'Royal Purple' 36
Crinum × powellii 67–8, *67*
Crocosmia 38
   × crocosmiiflora 68
   hybrids 68
   masonorum 37, 68
Crocus 15, 23, 32, 36, 41, 42, 47, 56, 68–72
   ancyrensis 71
   angustifolius 71
   autumn-flowering 21, 69–70
   banaticus 68, 69
   biflorus 71
   cancellatus 52, 69
   chrysanthus and vars 71
   corsicus 71–2
   dalmaticus 72
   etruscus 72
   flavus 72
   fleischeri 72
   goulimyi *68*, 69

   hadriaticus 69
   imperati 71, *72*
   kotschyanus 69
   laevigatus 69
   medius 69
   minimus 72
   niveus 69
   nudiflorus 69
   ochroleucus 69
   olivieri 72
   pulchellus 70
   sativus 70
   serotinus 70
   sieberi 72
   'Firefly' *70*
   speciosus 70
   spring-flowering 71–2
   tommasinianus 72
   tournefortii 70
   vernus 72
crown imperial, see Fritillaria imperialis
Curtonus 37
   paniculatus 71, 72–3
cutworms 50
Cyclamen 18, 36, 57
   cilicium 73
   coum 36, 73, *118*
   hederifolium (C. neapolitanum) 73, *73*
   purpurascens (C. europaeum) 73
   repandum 73
Cypella herbertii 73–4

Daffodil, see Narcissus
Dierama 25
   pulcherrimum 74, *74*
diseases 49–51
dividing 45–7, 47d
dog's-tooth violet, see Erythronium
Dracunculus vulgaris 74
drainage 27–8, 40

Endymion non-scripta 105
Eranthis hyemalis (Winter aconite) *26*, 47, 74
Erythronium 23, 27, 34, 41, 50, 56, 74–6
   dens-canis 74, *75*
   hendersonii 75
   oregonum 75
   revolutum 75
   tuolumnense 75–6, *75*
   'White Beauty' *23*
Eucomis 25, 43, 44
   bicolor 76
   comosa (E. punctata) *43*, 76
   undulata (E. autumnalis) 76
   zambesiaca 76

feeding 28, 32, 34–5, 41, 44, 56
fertilizers 34–5, 41, 44, 56
frames 28, 45d, 53
   beds in 56–7
   bulbs for 118

   pot cultivation in 54–6
Freesia 76
Fritillaria 76–8
   acmopetala 77
   camtschatcensis 77
   crassifolia 77
   graeca 77
   imperialis 15, 37, *50*, 76, 77
   lusitanica (F. hispanica) 77
   meleagris *58–9*, 77
   pallidiflora 77, *78*
   persica 77
   pontica 77
   pyrenaica 77–8
   raddeana 78
   uva-vulpis (F. assyriaca) 78
   verticillata 78
frost: protection from 43–4, 45d, 54
fungicides 38

Galanthus 18, *26*, 27, 34, 35, 36, 41, 47, 56, 78–9
   byzantinus 78
   caucasicus 35, 78
   cultivars 79
   elwesii 78
   ikariae 79
   latifolius 79
   nivalis 79
   plicatus 78
   reginae-olgae 79
Galtonia 25, 37, 43
   candicans 38, *79*, 79–80
Gladiolus 25, 28, 37, 80–1
   byzantinus *19*, 37, 80
   callianthus 38, *79*, 80
   colvillei 80
   communis 80
   cormlets 47d, 47
   hybrids 81, *81*
   italicus (G. segetum) 80
   nanus 80–1
   papilio 81
grape hyacinth, see Muscari
grass: bulbs in 31–3, 116
greenhouse, unheated 53
   beds in 56–7
   bulbs for 118
   pot cultivation in 54–6
grey mould 50–1

herbaceous perennials: bulbs with 36–8, 115
Herbert, William 16
Hermodactylus tuberosus 85
history 15–17
humus 35
Hyacinthoides non-scripta 105
Hyacinthus 15, 42, 47, 81–2, *82*
   azureus 93
hybridization 49

ink disease 51
Ipheion uniflorum 82

123

Index

Iris 15, 23, 56, 82–5
  bakeriana 83
  bucharica 83, 85
  danfordiae 83
  Dutch 37, 84
  English 37, 84
  graeberiana 85
  histrioides 33, 83, 117
  Juno group 84–5
  kolpakowskiana 16
  latifolia (*I. xiphioides*) 84
  magnifica 82, 85
  reticulata 41, 51, 51, 83–4
  Reticulata group 83–4
  Spanish 37, 84
  tuberosa 85
  winogradowii 84
  xiphium 84, 85
Ixia 85
Ixiolirion tataricum 85, 86

labelling 57
Leucojum (snowflake) 47, 50
  aestivum 20, 37, 86
  autumnale 86, 86
  nicaeense 86
  roseum 68
  vernum 86
lifting 27, 28, 38
Lilium 25, 28, 36, 37, 41, 42, 43, 44, 45, 51, 86–92
  amabile 87
  auratum 91–2
  canadense 87
  candidum 92
  carniolicum 87
  cernuum 87
  chalcedonicum 87–8
  concolor 92
  'Connecticut King' 45
  croceum 92
  dauricum 92
  davidii 88
  duchartrei 88
  'Enchantment' 91
  formosanum 90
  hansonii 88
  henryi 88, 89
  hybrids 90, 91, 92
  longiflorum 90
  mackliniae 88
  martagon 88
  maximowiczii 88
  monadelphum 88
  pardalinum 89
  pomponium 89
  propagation 48–9, 48d
  pumilum (*L. tenuifolium*) 89
  pyrenaicum 89
  regale 45, 90, 90
  speciosum 89–90
  superbum 89
  szovitsianum 88
  × *testaceum* 88
  tigrinum 90
lily beetles 50

Masson, Francis 17
Merendera montana 92–3, 92
Michaelmas daisy 37
Montbretia 37

Moraea:
  huttonii 93, 94
  moggii 93
  spathulata 93
mowers 33
Muscari 27, 32, 50, 58–9
  armeniacum 93, 94
  azureum 93
  botryoides 93
  comosum 93
  macrocarpum 93
  muscerimi (*M. moschatum*) 93–4
  neglectum (*M. racemosum*) 94
  tubergenianum 94
mutations 49

Narcissus 15, 27, 31, 32, 34, 35, 37, 39, 42, 47, 50
  asturiensis (*N. minimus*) 95
  bulbocodium 95
  canaliculatus 95
  cantabricus 95
  cyclamineus 95, 95–6
  Cyclamineus hybrids 96
  dwarf 56
  hybrids 29, 98
  jonquilla 96
  juncifolius 96
  lobularis 97
  papyraceus 97
  Poetaz group 96
  poeticus 96, 97
  pseudonarcissus 96–7
  rupicola 96
  scaberulus 96
  tazetta 96, 97
  triandrus 97
  watieri 98
narcissus flies 50
naturalizing 31–3
natural selection 18–19
Nectaroscordum:
  bulgaricum 98
  siculum (*N. dioscoridis*) 98
Nerine 21
  bowdenii 25, 98–9, 98
Nomocharis 25
  aperta 99
  mairei 99
  pardanthina 99–100, 99
  saluenensis 100

Orchids 18
Ornithogalum:
  arabicum 100
  balansae 100
  lanceolatum 100
  narbonense 100
  nutans 100
  pyrenaicum 100
  tenuifolium 101
  thrysoides 99, 100, 101
  umbellatum 27, 35, 101
Oxalis:
  adenophylla 101, 102
  enneaphylla 101
  laciniata 101
  tetraphylla (*O. deppei*) 101

Pancratium illyricum 101–2
Pentaglottis sempervirens 33

pests 49–51
planting: in grass 31–2, 32d, 33d
planting depth 32, 56, 57
plunging pots 44, 45d, 54
Polianthes tuberosa 25, 102
potash 32
  cultivation in 54–6
  in frame 53
  plunging 44, 45d, 54
  types 54
potting 54–6
propagation 45–9
Puschkinia scilloides 102, 102

rainfall:
  summer: bulbs needing 25
  winter: bulbs needing 21–4
Ranunculus 102–3
repotting 44–5, 54–6
Rhododendron 36
Rhodohypoxis 25, 41
  baurii 103, 103
rock gardens 28, 40–1, 117
Romulea bulbocodium 104, 104

Scilla 47
  autumnalis 104
  bifolia 104
  bithynica 104
  campanulata (*S. hispanica*) 104–5
  greilhuberi 105
  italica 105
  lilio-hyacinthus 105
  nutans (*S. non-scripta*) 105
  peruviana 105
  pratensis (*S. litardieri*) 105
  scilloides 105
  siberica 105
  tubergeniana 105
  verna 106
seed: propagation from 49
shrubs: bulbs with 28, 34–6, 116
sink: bulbs in 42
site 27–8
  for naturalizing 32
slugs 50
snakeshead fritillary 58–9, 77
snowflake, see *Leucojum*
soil 41
  improving 32
spacing 32
Sparaxis 106
staking 44
star of Bethlehem 27, 35, 101
Sternbergia 21, 41
  clusiana 106
  lutea 106, 106
  sicula 106
sulphate of potash 32
summer-growing bulbs:
  principles for growing 28
summer rainfall: bulbs needing 25

Tecophilaea 24
  cyanocrocus 106
Thunberg, Carl 17
Tigridia 38, 49
  pavonia 25, 37, 107, 107
top-dressing 35

trees: bulbs with 28, 34–6, 116
Trillium:
  erectum 108
  grandiflorum 107, 108
  rivale 108
  sessile (*T. cuneatum*) 108
Triteleia:
  hyacinthina 64
  ixioides 64
  laxa 64
tuber 13
tuberose 25, 102
Tulipa 15, 23, 37, 45, 49, 50, 108–12
  acuminata 109
  aucheriana 109, 110
  batalinii 109
  biflora 111
  chrysantha 109
  clusiana 109
  cornuta 14
  dwarf 41, 42
  eichleri 109
  fosteriana 22, 109, 112
  greigii 109, 110
  hageri 109, 111
  humilis 109
  hybrids 111–12
  kaufmanniana 110
  kolpakowskiana 110
  lily-flowered 30
  linifolia 110
  marjolettii 110
  maximowiczii 110
  praestans 110
  pulchella 109
  saxatilis 110
  sintenisii 10
  sprengeri 110–11
  stellata 109
  sylvestris 111
  tarda 111
  turkestanica 111
  urumiensis 111
  violacea 109
  'West Point' 30

ventilation 56, 57
Viburnum farreri (*V. fragrans*) 36
vine weevils 50
viruses 51

watering 44, 56, 57
Watsonia 112–13
  pyramidata (*W. rosea*) 113
  versveldii 113
  wordsworthiana 113
weedkillers 33
wild, bulbous plants in 21–5
window-boxes 42
Winter aconite, see *Eranthis hyemalis*
winter-growing bulbs: site 27–8
winter rainfall: bulbs needing 21–4

Zantedeschia aethiopica 113, 114
Zephyranthes candida 55, 113
Zigadenus elegans 113